D0364250

# MODERN *French* COOKING

# MODERN
## *French*
# COOKING

**ANDREAS ANTONA**

With forewords by Raymond Blanc and Richard Binns

Absolute Press

First published in Great Britain in 2006 by
**Absolute Press**
Scarborough House
29 James Street West
Bath BA1 2BT
Phone  44 (0) 1225 316013
Fax  44 (0) 1225 445836
E-mail  info@absolutepress.co.uk
Website  www.absolutepress.co.uk

Publisher: Jon Croft
Editor: Roz Denny
Design: Matt Inwood
Photography: Mark Law

A catalogue record of this book is
available from the British Library

**ISBN: 190457355X**
**ISBN 13: 9781904573555**

Printed and bound by Butler and Tanner,
Frome, Somerset

**A note about the text**
This book is set in Sabon MT and
Helvetica Neue. Sabon was designed by
Jan Tschichold in 1964. The roman design
is based on type by Claude Garamond,
whereas the italic design is based on types
by Robert Granjon. Helvetica was designed
in 1957 by Max Miedinger of the Swiss-
based Haas foundry. In the early 1980s,
Linotype redrew the entire Helvetica
family. The result was Helvetica Neue.

# Contents

# Forewords

*I first met Andreas 15 years ago and what really struck me about him was his incredible drive and determination. It comes as no surprise that he is now established as the successful owner of two distinguished restaurants in the West Midlands.*

A proud second generation Greek Cypriot, Andreas and his wife Alison had always wanted to own their own restaurant. Simpsons in Kenilworth, a fine dining French establishment, opened in 1993 and within six years won a Michelin star.
In 2004 Andreas transferred Simpsons to Edgbaston; it includes four stylish bedrooms and a cookery school all located within a magnificent, Grade II listed building.

Beyond his success as a chef and restaurateur, Andreas also makes a considerable contribution to promoting young chefs and culinary awareness in the West Midlands. In the last decade Andreas has nurtured exceptional talent such as Glyn Purnell of Jessica's and Andy Waters of Edmunds and his own executive chef Luke Tipping who has been with him for over 15 years, man and boy. The pinnacle of Andreas' conscientious efforts was the launch of the Midlands Chef of the Year, which he created six years ago to admirable acclaim. Looking beyond Britain, Andreas used his position as a Governor of the Birmingham College of Food, Tourism and Creative Studies to influence the twinning of Birmingham with Lyon in 1998. This firmly placed Birmingham alongside the leading home of gastronomy and has created opportunities for placements among young British chefs to work in the Lyon region.

This recipe book encompasses the very essence of what Andreas and his team have achieved at Simply Simpsons in Kenilworth and Simpsons in Edgbaston. Chefs' recipe books can often be intimidating, but inside this book you will find essential and relatively easy restaurant recipes that will make excellent choices for entertaining at home.

Warm congratulations to Andreas and his team.

*Raymond Blanc, June 2006*

*I first tested Andreas' cooking skills over 20 years ago when he was at the Dorchester working for Anton Mossiman. Since 1993, when he opened his own restaurant, Simpsons, a few miles from my home, I have had the good fortune to discover why Andreas is such a talented, organised and superb man-manager chef.*

The son of a restaurateur, Sussex-born Andreas' culinary C.V. had left him wonderfully equipped to show off his abilities at Simpsons in Kenilworth: first spells in both Switzerland and Germany; back in London working at both the Dorchester and the Ritz; and then in the Midlands' best hotel restaurants. The essential base of mastering classical cuisine techniques had been complemented by the chance to absorb innovative modern cooking ways.

What makes Andreas especially important as a chef have been his prodigious efforts to ratchet-up cooking standards in the Midlands. His work with the Birmingham College of Food (he's now a governor of the latter) and the 'second-city' hands-on training links he's developed with the chefs of Lyon have produced truly rich dividends. Equally important have been the myriad youngsters who have started their careers with Andreas during the last 20 years – and have gone on to becoming super chefs in their own right, working for him, opening their own businesses (two with their own Michelin stars), or finding success in other restaurants.

Young men like Luke Tipping, Andy Waters, Glynn Purnell, Adam Bennet, Simon Morris and Iain Miller are just six that come to mind. They, in turn, in a cascade effect, will pass on their skills to many others. No-one in the Midlands has done more to improve both cooking and restaurant standards than Andreas.

*Richard Binns, July 2006*

# Beginnings

# Early Years

*'Right from an early stage, all I wanted to do was become a chef.'*

Right from an early stage, all I wanted to do was become a chef. My other dream was to be a footballer (like another top UK celebrity chef!) but at the end of the day, I wasn't good enough. My mum and dad are Greek Cypriots so I consider myself to be a Greek Cypriot, and I'm proud of it! I got my love for cooking from my dad. He was a perfectionist in everything he did, and I suppose I grew up with this as an ethos.

When dad arrived in the UK at the age of 17 in 1947, he joined a family-run catering business in London's Regent Street. He worked hard, saved his money and eventually he and his brother bought a restaurant in Bayswater, west London. He had married my mum by then and one of my earliest memories is living above the restaurant and hearing the sounds of chefs banging around in the kitchen and catching the smells of good cooking wafting up the stairs.

Our household was always busy – invariably with something on the stove. Big bowls of macaroni, dishes like *Kleftiko*, *Tavas*, *Stifado* – real country cooking. My aunts and uncles would grow vegetables that weren't then common in the UK, like aubergines, courgettes and rocket leaves for salads. They also reared rabbits and pigeons, not as pets, but for the pot. They would go back to Cyprus for holidays and return with Haloumi cheese, *bastoumas* or *loukanikas* – so for me, it was really like growing up in Cyprus, even though we were actually in Isleworth.

At home, my mum and dad spoke Greek most of the time. My generation – sisters, cousins, and other visitors would speak English, but my grandmother, who lived in this country for 55 years, never learnt to speak any English even though she used to enjoy watching Coronation Street.

*'Our household was always busy – invariably with something on the stove. My aunts and uncles would grow vegetables that weren't then common in the UK, like aubergines, courgettes and rocket leaves for salads. They also reared rabbits and pigeons, not as pets, but for the pot.'*

One of my happiest memories of being a kid was the weekend – sitting around a big table at my grandmother's house with my extended family for Sunday lunch. It was a long, drawn out affair which would last all day with several breaks when the women would chat and the men play cards. Starters would be stuffed vine leaves or some soup. Main course, lamb or chicken and lots of vegetables. And so on into late evening when we would eventually tuck into a big fruit platter.

The Greek way of life was that girls would stay at home with mum and the sons follow their dad. So from a very early age I would wander down to my dad's restaurant after school finished to slice mushrooms and wash plates. When any of the chefs went away on holiday, I'd take my place on the griddle. From the age of 14 years I was boning out ribs of beef and legs of pork.

I was lucky that my uncle owned the only major Greek delicatessen in west London. It was a massive shop called T.A. Adamou & Sons Ltd. on Chiswick High Road. It would usually be full of Greeks and Jamaicans, buying pickled pigs' ears and pigs' tails – and later on when the Arabs came into London, he would stock all the Arab and Lebanese specialities for them. It is still a Mecca for dedicated foodies.

*'...from a very early age, I would wander down to my dad's restaurant after school finished to slice mushrooms and wash plates. When any of the chefs went away on holiday, I'd take my place on the griddle. From the age of 14 years I was boning out ribs of beef and legs of pork.'*

Back then in the mid-1960s a plane would arrive once a week loaded with Greek goodies for the supermarkets but my uncle's shop was always the first stop for the delivery guys. Foods like Greek cucumbers, cherries, figs, tiger melons – all of these things which might seem normal now but weren't back then. And I grew up with them, I could tell if a melon was ripe from the age of 5 years old.

# Early Days and My Mentors

When we first opened Simpsons, my dad would come to Birmingham market with me and sift through 10 boxes of aubergines to make up just one box that made his grade. In Mediterranean countries the locals hand-pick their food. They rub, look, and smell before buying. I do that at my local supermarket and my wife mutters 'Here we go again'.

I trained at Ealing College where I learnt the disciplines of a structured classical French cuisine. It is a firm foundation on which I draw on constantly. After college I worked in Europe – first in Switzerland starting in a restaurant on the concourse of Zurich station. After that I moved onto Germany and the Stuttgart International Hotel. It was here that I first heard about the great Anton Mosimann, then 29 years old, who had started a new revolution in London's Dorchester Hotel. I knew I wanted to go back and be part of this new revolution and fortunately my boss let me go.

Mosimann is still an innovator and a world player and I feel honoured to have been one of his 'boys'. He had a respect for the ingredients more than anyone else I have worked with and from him I learnt to prepare dishes with a lighter touch. Before Mosimann, for example, stodgy roux-based sauces would have been pre-cooked in the morning and reheated. Mosimann's new way was light, creamy and buzzing with flavour. I had an immediate attraction and an affinity to this style of cooking.

*'Mosimann is still an innovator and a world player and I feel honoured to have been one of his 'boys'.'*

But there came a time when I decided it was in my best interest to move on – and that move was just a short walk down the road to The Ritz, to work under the legendary English chef Michael Quinn. The Ritz, in those days was old and decrepit. The outside looked great for the customers and guests, but behind the scenes, it left a lot to be desired. I also found that I was cooking food that was still 10 years behind what Mosimann was doing. But I was lucky to be working with some great young chefs who have since gone on and blazed great trails throughout the UK. We revived the Ritz's fortunes and helped to make it one of the finest Hotel restaurants in Europe. We were the talk of the town. Being a chef with Ritz training, in those days, was a passport to success – we were always in demand.

Michael Quinn was the first real celebrity chef – he became a superstar. He was English born and bred, and no other Englishman had been recognised as a top-quality chef at this level before Michael. He was a great motivator, and another inspirational character. I still see him on a regular basis 20 years later.

# The Simpson's Story

Like all big establishments, staff came and went at the Ritz, but one day I spotted a young lass called Alison working as second commis chef. It was the start of a romance that has lasted 20 years and coincided with me moving out of London eventually to set up my own business.

Alison and I started in Kenilworth in 1993. We started small and had our share of ups and downs. For a start it took us over a year to find the right premises in the heart of Kenilworth, a location that had once been a chemist's shop, owned by Alison's father. It was called Simpson's and we decided to keep the name.

It needed quite a lot of work doing to it – but I'm delighted to say, that it appeared to be successful as soon as we opened the doors. A good friend said when we opened up, 'Full restaurants make money; empty ones don't.' I thought there was a lot of truth in that and have always tried to get the quality right, the food right and the service right. One of the things we have always agreed on is a hospitable welcome and with Alison running the front of house, we could at least be sure of that. Luke Tipping joined us after about three months and is still here today – an excellent Head Chef.

The early menus featured dishes such as *Grilled Haloumi Cheese* and *Kleftiko* (braised shank of lamb), which is still on the menu today. I don't keep it on, the customers do! It was a childhood dish that my mum used to cook. I think I cook it better than she used to, but her style of cooking and technique was geared for the family. We cook it for the restaurant market and use a better quality lamb from Cornwall.

> *The early menus featured dishes such as* Grilled Haloumi Cheese *and* Kleftiko *(braised shank of lamb), which is still on the menu today.*

I'm lucky to have a good team working with me at Simpsons. When I take on new staff, I not only give them a good knowledge of the trade, but also try to develop them into better people. It's all in their attitude – they have to want to be here and be very dedicated to the trade. If not, we're all wasting our time.

The menu at Simpsons today has evolved over the years and I suppose my repertoire is a direct result of the time I spent at The Dorchester and The Ritz. My style of cooking has come from the things I learnt whilst working with Mosimann. He was one of the first chefs to make food look pretty on a plate. But not just pretty, he was worried about getting the flavours right as well. When we change the menu here, we often come up with a dish and I'll think back – how would Mosimann do this? His style and influence is still with me to this day!

In October 2004, after eleven happy years in Kenilworth, Simpsons relocated to a beautiful Georgian Grade II listed site in Edgbaston, Birmingham and, retaining its Michelin star in January 2005, becoming the only Michelin-starred restaurant with rooms in Britain's second city. It is hard to believe that with its lovely garden views and orangery, the new restaurant is just one mile from the city centre of Birmingham. With four individually styled luxury bedrooms and a newly launched cookery demonstration school I hope to build on Birmingham as a culinary centre of excellence.

# So, Why a Book?

For some time now, customers and friends have been buying me copies of other people's cookery books or collections of recipes and asking, 'Why don't you do one?' I think you have to have a clear vision of what you want to achieve out of a book like this and when I really thought about it, I felt that the experiences I have lived through and the influences I have adopted might well be worth putting into print. So here it is!

Fundamentally, the world of a chef is a very narrow subjective little world. I look at myself as a craftsmen – not a scientist or an artist. There is not much of a mystery in this job – customers come in, we cook the food and serve it to them. They decide if they've had value for their money and then whether they'll come back again.

So, we must always remember that we're only as good as our last meal! It doesn't matter how good the chef's reputation is, if he's not doing the job properly, it's back to square one – it's that basic!

This book attempts to explain the way we cook the dishes at Simpsons in a way that will enable you to cook them at home with ease. The dishes are set out in what I hope is an easy-to-follow style and I'm sure you will enjoy trying many of these out for yourself – but if you'd prefer someone else to do all the work (and the washing-up!) then don't forget – we're here to cook it for you at Simpsons in Edgbaston or Kenilworth.

*Fundamentally, the world of a chef is a very narrow subjective little world. I look at myself as a craftsmen – not a scientist or an artist.*

*Andreas Antona,*
*Birmingham, July 2006*

The Team: (L–R) Matt Cheal, Luke Tipping, Andreas Antona, Adam Bennett

# Basics

# Wholemeal Bread

*We make all our own bread at the restaurant and shape the dough into small rolls. The recipe we use is very versatile allowing us to mix in different seeds to vary flavours and textures.*

Makes 2 large loaves or 1 loaf and 20 rolls

*50g fresh yeast*
*500g strong plain flour*
*250g wholemeal flour*
*250g Granary flour*
*3 teaspoons fine sea salt*

*2 teaspoons caster sugar*
*100g butter, softened*
*Optional – 100g mix of seeds and*
  *grains – linseeds, hemp, sesame,*
  *pumpkin, sunflower, caraway*

Crumble the yeast into 550ml tepid water and stir until dissolved. Mix together the flours, salt and sugar in a large mixing bowl. Rub in the butter and stir in the seeds and grains, if using.

Make a well in the centre and add the yeasty water. Stir well together to a smooth dough, adding extra dribbles of tepid water if necessary. This can be done in a large electric mixer but not a food processor.

Turn out the dough onto a worktop and knead with your hands for a good 10 minutes. No need to add extra flour, the dough will become less sticky the more you knead. Shape into a smooth ball and return to the original bowl. Cover with Clingfilm then leave to rise in a warm place until doubled in volume. This should take anything from 2–4 hours.

Punch the dough down and turn out again to knead for a minute or so. Divide into two. Shape either into two rectangles and drop into lightly greased non-stick 1 kg loaf tins, or make 1 loaf and roll the other half of dough into 20 smooth balls. Place the balls on a non-stick baking sheet. Snip the dough into peaks or slash once or twice as crosses. Cover again loosely with greased Clingfilm and leave the balls and/or loaves to prove until doubled again in volume.

Meanwhile, preheat the oven to 220°C, Gas 7. Place a large roasting pan of boiling water on a lower shelf and place the loaves and/or rolls on the upper shelf. Bake rolls for 8–10 minutes and whole loaves for 20–25 minutes. The loaves are cooked when they sound hollow tapped on the base after turning out. Cool on a wire rack.

## To knead like a professional

Shape the dough into a long oval and holding each end make a scrubbing action as if washing clothes! Then after 30 seconds or so, gather the dough into an oval and repeat again and again.

# Olive Oil Foccacia with Maldon Salt

Serves 6–8

500g strong plain flour, plus extra
  for kneading
1¹/₂ teaspoons Maldon salt, crushed
  plus extra for baking
50g butter

225ml tepid water
20g fresh yeast or 1 sachet easy-
  blend yeast
3–4 tablespoons extra virgin olive
  oil

In a large bowl, mix together the flour and salt. Rub in the butter. If using fresh yeast then blend with the water. If using easy-blend, mix into the flour after the butter.

Stir in the water and mix to a dough with a smooth elastic texture. Turn the dough out onto a lightly floured board, and knead for about 10 minutes by hand. If doing this in a machine with a dough hook, allow 5 minutes. If the dough seems dry then add extra water in cautious dribbles, it all depends on the flour.

Cover the dough with Clingfilm and leave to rise in a warm place until doubled in size. This can take up to 2–3 hours.

Knock back (i.e. punch down) the dough and turn out onto a worktop and knead lightly for a minute or so.

Lightly oil a shallow rectangle ovenproof tin, about 15 x 25cm and 5cm deep. Roll out the dough to fit and press lightly in. It doesn't have to fit exactly. Cover again with Clingfilm (lightly greased) and leave to prove in a warm place until doubled in size.

Preheat the oven to 190°C, Gas 5. Uncover the dough, and using your finger tips prod several times. Drizzle with the oil and crush over 1–2 teaspoons more salt. Bake for 12–15 minutes until risen and golden brown. Cool then turn out onto a wire rack until cold. Serve cut in slices or squares.

## Alternative flavours

Instead of crushed salt flakes on top you could add quarters of cherry tomatoes or slivers of garlic, or fennel seeds, crushed dried sage leaves or snipped rosemary leaves.

# Pain d'Epice

*Pain d'Epice is a spiced bread we bake in Simpsons that has many uses and keeps well, rather like gingerbread. We also like to add small cubes of it to Pain d'Epice ice cream and grill crisp triangles as a decoration.*

*50g caster sugar*
*120g rye flour*
*120g plain lour*
*20g baking powder*
*2 teaspoons mixed spice*
*2 teaspoons ground ginger*

*Grated zest $1/_2$ lemon*
*Grated zest $1/_2$ orange*
*250g clear honey, warmed*
*125 ml milk*
*3 free range eggs, beaten*
*2 teaspoons vanilla extract*

Grease and line a 1kg loaf tin. Heat the oven to 150°C, Gas 2.

Mix the dry ingredients in a large mixing bowl including the grated zests.

Make a well in the centre and pour in the honey, milk, eggs and extract then beat well together until smooth.

Pour into the prepared tin and bake in the centre of the oven for about $1^1/_2$ hours until firm on top when pressed. You can double check that it is cooked by sticking a thin metal skewer in the middle which should come out clean.

Remove and cool in the tin for 30 minutes then shake out onto a wire rack. When cold, wrap in Clingfilm and store in an airtight container. The loaf will keep for around 4 days like this or can be frozen in slices.

## To measure honey easily

Heat the jar (without a metal lid) in a microwave oven on low until it is runny or place the jar in a shallow pan of simmering water. Then pour the honey directly into a pan or mixing bowl to weigh.

# Pasta Dough

*It is best to make a full quantity of this recipe as you will find it much easier to handle a larger amount of dough. Leftover dough freezes well either in a ball or cut into noodles.*

Makes about 800g

*550g plain flour*
*¹/₂ teaspoon fine sea salt*
*4 medium freerange eggs*

*6 egg yolks*
*2 tablespoons olive oil*

Place all the ingredients into a food processor and pulse until they form into clumps. Turn out onto a worktop and knead with your hands to a smooth dough that is soft but not sticky.

Wrap in Clingfilm and rest for an hour or so. Divide the dough into 8 and roll each piece on a lightly floured worktop to 3mm thick rectangle (thickness of a £1 coin).

Feed each rectangle through a pasta machine several times starting with the thickest setting and finishing with the thinnest.

The pasta is now ready for use. For filled shapes, e.g. tortellini, use the pasta just rolled; for cutting into noodles etc allow the sheets to dry slightly so they cut cleanly.

# Gremolata

Makes about 80g

*100g flat leaf parsley*
*1 clove garlic, roughly chopped*
*Grated zest 1 lemon*

*About 3 tablespoons olive oil*
*Sea salt and freshly ground black*
 *pepper*

Pick off the leaves of the parsley and place in a food processor or blender with the garlic and lemon zest.

Blitz for at least a minute gradually drizzling in the oil until you have a rough purée. Season with salt and pepper. Store in a clean screw topped jar and use as required. Chill until ready to use. Keeps for up to one week

# Pesto

*Homemade pesto has an infinitely better taste than ready made and is so easy to make that there really is no excuse for resorting to shop bought. Ideally, make it the original way in a pestle and mortar for a rougher texture, but if you are feeling lazy you can always whizz it together in a liquidiser.*

Serves 4

*1 clove garlic, peeled*
*50g basil leaves*
*25g pine nuts, grilled or toasted*

*5 tablespoons freshly grated Parmesan*
*120ml extra virgin olive oil*
*Sea salt and freshly ground pepper*

In a mortar crush the garlic to a purée with a pinch of salt. Add the basil and pine nuts and crush to a smooth paste.

Add the Parmesan then trickle in the olive oil in a steady stream, stirring continuously with the pestle. Work the sauce until smooth then season lightly again.

Use immediately or cover and chill for up to a week.

# Aubergine Caviar

*This is an excellent way to treat aubergines and makes a very nice accompaniment for lamb and fish.*

Serves 4–6

*1 large aubergine*
*1 clove garlic, crushed*
*1 small sprig fresh rosemary*
*Some olive oil*

*1 large shallot, finely chopped*
*10g basil leaves, chopped*
*Sea salt and freshly ground black*
  *pepper*

Cut the aubergines in half and score the flesh of both halves. Spread garlic down one half and place the rosemary on top. Sprinkle with some oil then sandwich together the two halves and wrap tightly in foil.

Bake at 190°C, Gas 5 and bake for about 1 hour or until the aubergine collapses right down and the flesh feels very soft when pierced. Remove and cool.

Meanwhile, sauté the shallot in about 2 tablespoons of oil until softened. Unwrap the aubergine, discard the garlic and rosemary and scrape the flesh onto a board and chop the flesh. Discard the skin.

Cook gently for about 10 minutes until the mixture is pasty, then mix in the chopped basil. Season and set aside. Cool and use as required.

# Crispy Parsley Leaves

*An eye-catching garnish.*

Pick out a good handful of flat leaf parsley leaves. Wash and pat dry. Cover a dinner plate tightly with Clingfilm, stretching taut like a drum. Place the leaves on in a single layer, brush lightly with oil and cook on full power in a microwave for 2–3 minutes until crisp and bright green. Leave to cool and the leaves will crisp. Store in an air tight container.

# Tapenade

*You can store this irresistable olive paste in a screw topped jar in the fridge.*

Makes about 200g

*200g pitted black olives*
*100ml olive oil*

*30g capers*
*5 anchovy fillets*

Place all ingredients in a blender, blend for 3–5 minutes until smooth and rub through a fine sieve with the back of a ladle.

# Parmesan Tuiles

*These are so easy it's embarrassing! All you need is grated cheese.*

Makes about 10

*50g Parmesan cheese, finely grated*

Heat the oven to 160°C, Gas 3. Line a flat baking sheet with non-stick baking parchment or a Silpat mat. Place a round cutter on top, around 5–6cm, and sprinkle in a light layer of cheese.

Repeat several times over the sheet. Bake 8–10 minutes until golden and melted. Remove from the oven, cool a few seconds then scoop onto a wire tray to crisp.

# Sesame Tuiles

Simply sprinkle the cheese with sesame seeds before baking. Also, good sprinkled with coarsely ground black pepper.

# Chicory Marmalade

Serves 4

4 large heads of chicory
1 large (banana) shallot
A good knob of butter
1 sprig fresh tarragon
1 thick parsley stalk
2 tablespoons sherry vinegar

2 tablespoons white wine vinegar
1 slightly rounded tablespoon caster
  sugar
1 teaspoon sea salt
Freshly ground black pepper

Using the tip of a small sharp knife, hollow out the cores of the chicory. Slice each in half lengthways and shred finely.

Finely slice the shallot lengthways and sweat off with the butter for about 5 minutes.

Add the herb sprigs, vinegars, sugar and seasoning. Stir in the chicory. Cook on a moderate heat until the leaves are soft and the liquor has been reduced. Remove the tarragon and parsley and serve.

# Garlic Confit

*Use olive oil to make the confit when accompanying with fish dishes or general use, and duck fat for meat dishes.*

2 heads garlic with large cloves,
  ideally rose-skinned
About 200ml olive oil or duck fat

2 sprigs fresh thyme
1 bay leaf

Separate the cloves from the stem but do not peel.

Place in a saucepan and cover with the oil, ensuring the cloves are submerged. Add the herbs.

Cook on a very low heat, stirring occasionally until the cloves feel soft when pressed, about 30 minutes, then remove and cool in the oil. Store in a screw topped jar until required. The garlics can be popped from the skins or served whole.

# Semi-Dried Confit Tomatoes

*10 ripe plum tomatoes*                    *2 tablespoons olive oil*
*2 cloves garlic, sliced thinly*           *1 teaspoon sea salt*
*10 sprigs fresh thyme, leaves only*       *1 teaspoon caster sugar*

Blanch the tomatoes in a large pan of boiling water for just 6 seconds then plunge into a bowl of iced water for a minute. Drain, peel, halve and scoop out the seeds, then pat dry with paper towel.

Heat an oven to the lowest setting, around 90–100°C, Gas Low. Lay out the tomatoes cut side up in a tray. Dot with the garlic slices, scatter over the thyme leaves, then the oil, salt and sugar.

Bake for up to 2 hours until the flesh shrinks back a little and feels tender. Remove and cool. Store in the fridge until required.

# Lemon Confit

*A wonderfully versatile garnish for sweet and savoury dishes alike.*

*3 large un-waxed lemons*                  *300g caster sugar*

Wash the lemons and then slice as thinly as possible.

Dissolve the sugar in a large saucepan with 500ml of water. When clear bring to the boil and press in the lemon slices.

Simmer very gently for about 5 minutes then remove the pan from the heat and allow the contents to cool.

Store the lemons and syrup in a large screw topped jar and keep chilled until required. When finished, the syrup can be used to flavour fruit salads, etc.

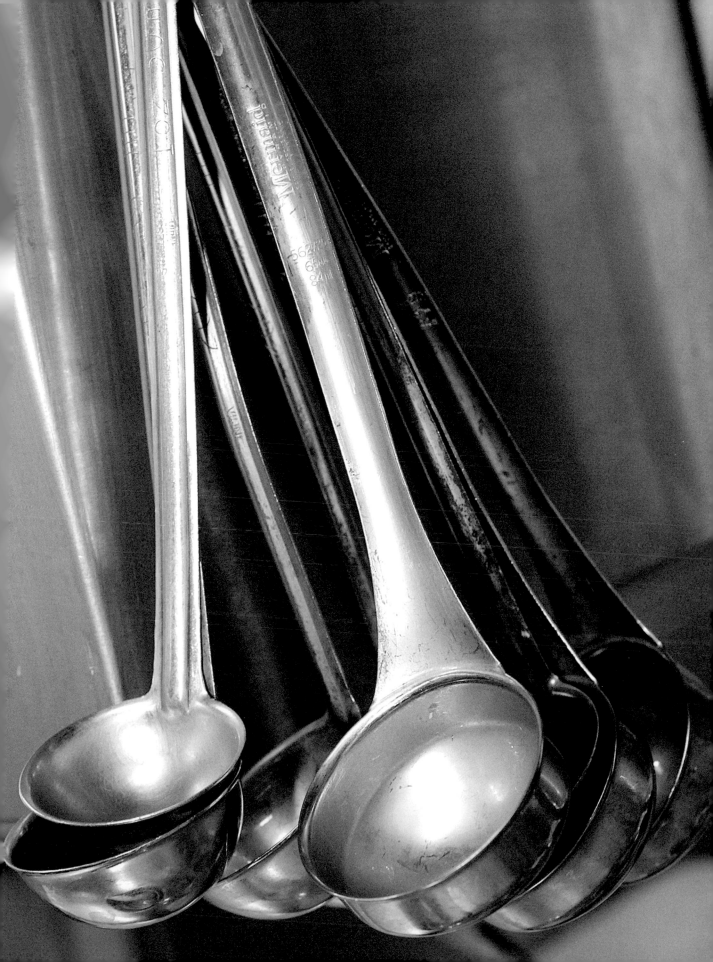

# Stocks and Jus

The secret of success in my dishes lies in using well-prepared stocks made from wholesome ingredients, patiently allowing time for them to simmer and reduce slowly, extracting every last gram of natural flavour.

I appreciate that in a restaurant kitchen we make fresh stock every day and so stirring in a jug or glass or even splash of stock is easy for us. Fresh stock does keep well in the fridge or freezer, so why not make up batches and freeze in smaller useable portions? They can be cooked from frozen anyway, melting in minutes, and make such a difference to a dish.

Remember, you need to boil down stock until it is reduced by up to three quarters the original volume. And no seasoning – that comes later.

Jus is my term for a stock made from a specific meat that has been boiled down to a rich glossy liquid which some chefs call a 'demi-glace'. They can be used instead of the rich elaborate sauces that used to be the norm in the heady days of 'haute cuisine'. Again, make up a batch and freeze what you don't use first time round in ice cubes making a note of the flavour and quantities. Many of the flavours are interchangeable. As a rough guide we normally reckon about 50ml (that's a generous 3 tablespoons) of well-flavoured jus per serving.

## Hints on stock making and storage

Always aim for a clear, bright stock. For that reason, once the water has come to the boil, turn the heat to a simmer – don't boil.

Reduce stocks down by just over half – so 2.5 litres of water will give you a well-flavoured single litre of stock.

For the same reason, skim stocks of any foam or scum that rises to the top during cooking. This is a harmless foam of proteins and mild impurities. Regular skimming gives a clear stock.

After cooking, allow the pan and liquid to settle for about 10 minutes then carefully pour off the liquid leaving any debris undisturbed at the bottom. I use a conical fine mesh sieve to pour the liquid through. If you have one, you could also line this with a wet clean piece of muslin or a new J-Cloth.

Don't add salt during cooking. There is a lot of natural salt in the bones, vegetables, etc. already. You can always add a little salt right at the end, although personally I wait until I use the stock in a dish to check seasoning.

Many recipes in this book call for about 200–250ml of stock, so I suggest you freeze them in those quantities. Cool then pour into small freezer proof containers then demould when frozen and bag. Make sure you label them with the flavour because it's amazing how a chicken stock can look like fish or veal or vegetable!

# Chicken Stock

Makes 1 litre

1 chicken, ideally a boiling fowl, weighing 1.5kg or an equal weight of fresh chicken carcasses or wings
2 medium carrots, cut into chunks
White part of 2 leeks, cut into chunks
1 celery stalk, coarsely chopped
1 onion
150g button mushrooms, thinly sliced
1 bouquet garni – a large bay leaf, thyme sprig, rosemary sprig and some parsley stalks tied together

Put the chicken or carcasses in a saucepan and cover with 2.5 litres cold water. Bring to the boil over high heat, then immediately lower the heat and keep at a simmer.

After 5 minutes, skim the surface using a slotted spoon then add all the other ingredients. Cook gently for $1^1/_2$ hours, without boiling, skimming every half hour, or as necessary, until you have about 1 litre.

Strain the stock through a wire-mesh conical sieve, which can be lined with a wet muslin cloth, and cool it as quickly as possible.

# Poultry or Game Bird Jus

*e.g. Chicken, Guinea Fowl, Pigeon, etc.*

Makes about 250ml

*1 tablespoon ground nut or olive oil*
*500g chicken, guinea fowl or pigeon*
*    trimmings*
*1 shallot, chopped*
*100ml white wine*

*500ml chicken stock*
*1 sprig of thyme*
*Sea salt and freshly ground black*
*    pepper*

Heat the oil in a large pan. Add the poultry trimmings and fry vigorously until all browned. Strain off excess oil from the pan and add the shallots. Stir together and cook for 1 minute and then add the white wine. Boil and reduce down by half.

Add the stock and thyme and simmer until reduced by half again. Pass through a fine sieve and season. Keep warm for serving.

# Fish Stock

*White fish trimmings make the best stock. Ask your fishmonger for the bones of soles, brill, turbot or whiting if you don't have enough. If using fish heads, than remove the eyes with a thin pointed knife and the gills with kitchen scissors. Don't be tempted to use any fish skin or bones from oily fish, including salmon.*

Makes 1 litre

*1.5kg bones and trimmings of*
*    white fish (e.g. sole, turbot, brill,*
*    Whiting), roughly chopped pieces*
*50g butter*
*White of 2 leeks, thinly sliced*
*$^1/_2$ medium onion, thinly sliced*

*75g button mushrooms, thinly sliced*
*200ml dry white wine*
*1 bouquet garni*
*2 slices of lemon*
*1 clove garlic*
*8 white peppercorns*

Rinse the fish bones and trimmings under cold running water then drain.

In a large saucepan, melt the butter and sweat the vegetables over low heat for a few minutes. Add the fish bones and trimmings, sauté gently for a few moments, then pour in the wine.

Cook until reduced by two-thirds, and then add 2.5 litres cold water. Bring to the boil, lower the heat, skim the surface with a slotted spoon and add the bouquet garni, lemon slices, garlic and peppercorns. Simmer very gently for 25 minutes, skimming as necessary. Turn off the heat and leave to infuse a further 10 minutes. Gently ladle the stock through a fine-mesh conical sieve and cool it as quickly as possible.

# Lobster Stock

Makes 1 litre

1 lobster head, raw
3 tablespoons olive oil
1 small onion, chopped
2 red peppers, cored and chopped

5 tomatoes, chopped
1 sprig of fresh basil
A few Parma ham trimmings,
  optional

Crush the lobster head with a rolling pin or meat bat. Heat the oil in a large sauce pan and fry the head over a high heat until lightly coloured.

Add the onion and red peppers and continue to cook vigorously for 5 minutes, then add the tomatoes and cook for a further 10 minutes.

Add the basil and Parma ham, if using, and cover with about 2 litres of cold water or Chicken Stock (page 29). Bring to the boil then lower the heat and simmer gently, uncovered, for 1 hour. Strain through a sieve, ideally lined with wet muslin, cool and chill.

Use as required or freeze in two 500ml blocks.

# Veal Stock

*Veal bones give a good all-round body and flavour to a sauce be it meat, poultry or even fish. Veal bones can be found at quality high street butchers. They need to be chopped up to fit into a large home saucepan. Chopping the bones also releases the bone marrow adding extra flavour and goodness.*

Makes about 500ml (freeze in 4 or 5 batches)

2.5kg veal bones, chopped roughly
1 large carrot
$^{1}/_{2}$ onion
2 sticks celery
4 cloves garlic

A little olive oil
250ml white wine
500g tomatoes
400g mushrooms
1 large sprig fresh thyme

Heat the oven to 220°C, Gas 7. Put the bones into a large roasting pan and roast for about 25 minutes until nicely browned. Tip into a large stock pan.

Roughly chop the carrot, onion, celery and garlic then add to the roasting pan drizzling with a little oil, if necessary. Roast for about 15 minutes until lightly browned, stirring once or twice. Tip into the pot, leaving the oil behind.

Pour in the white wine and cook until reduced by half then pour in enough water to cover by about 7cm (about 5 litres). Bring to the boil and simmer until reduced down by a third.

Chop the tomatoes and mushrooms and pop into the pot with the thyme. Return to a very gentle simmer and cook for at least 2 hours until you have about 1 litre of stock remaining. (In the restaurant kitchen we cook stock six times this amount, and simmer our stock for up to 8 hours).

Remove the pan from the heat and allow to stand for 30 minutes and then gently pour off the rich stock straining it through a muslin lined sieve. Divide into 4 to 5 batches, chill and freeze what you don't need immediately.

# Veal Jus

*Possibly the most useful jus there is.*

*800ml veal stock*

Boil the strained stock down by three quarters until you have about 200 ml. This is what we use as a light well-flavoured serving sauce.

# Vegetable Stock

*Vegetarians – no need to despair! It is easy to make a good rich stock using a medley of vegetables.*

Makes 1 litre

*3 medium carrots, cut into rounds*
*White part of 2 leeks, thinly sliced*
*2 celery sticks, thinly sliced*
*1/4 bulb fennel, very thinly sliced*
*3 shallots, thinly sliced*
*1 medium onion, thinly sliced*
*2 unpeeled garlic cloves*

*1 bouquet garni – a large bay leaf,*
*thyme sprig, rosemary sprig and*
*some parsley stalks tied together*
*250ml dry white wine*
*10 white peppercorns, crushed and*
*wrapped in muslin*

Put all the ingredients in a saucepan. Add 2 litres of cold water. Bring to the boil over high heat, then cook at a bare simmer for 35 minutes, skimming as necessary until reduced by half and you have around 1 litre of liquid.

Strain through a fine-mesh conical sieve into a bowl and cool as quickly as possible.

# Lamb Stock

*Because we serve a lot of lamb dishes in Simpsons, we use this well-flavoured lamb stock for extra luxury.*

Makes 1 litre

*1.5kg scrag end, breast or lower best end of lamb, skin and fat removed, chopped into pieces*
*2 carrots, cut into rounds*
*1 medium onion, coarsely chopped*
*250ml dry white wine*
*4 tomatoes, peeled, deseeded and chopped*
*2 garlic cloves*
*1 bouquet garni, including 2 sprigs of tarragon and a celery stalk*
*6 white peppercorns, crushed and wrapped in muslin*

Preheat the oven to 220°C, Gas 7. Put the pieces of lamb in a roasting pan and brown in the hot oven, turning them over from time to time with a slotted spoon. When the lamb has coloured, add the carrots and onions then cook for another 5 minutes.

Still using the slotted spoon, transfer all the contents of the roasting pan to a large saucepan or stock pot. Pour off the fat from the roasting pan and place the pan over a hob burner. Pour in the wine and bubble up, scraping the meaty deposits. Cook for about 3 minutes until reduced by half.

Pour the reduced wine into the saucepan, add 2.5 litres cold water and bring to the boil over high heat. As soon as the liquid boils, reduce the heat so that the surface is barely trembling. Simmer for 10 minutes, then skim the surface and add all the other ingredients.

Simmer, uncovered, for $1^{1}/_{2}$ hours, skimming the surface as necessary until you have around 1 litre. Strain the stock through a fine-mesh conical sieve into a bowl and cool it as quickly as possible.

# Lamb Jus

*This is a quicker light serving sauce.*

Take about 300–500g of lamb meat trimmings. Heat a heavy based pan with a little oil and fry the lamb with 2 shallots, roughly chopped. Keep stirring and cooking until the meat and shallots turn dark brown then pour in about 400ml lamb stock. Season and simmer until the liquid is reduced by a good half to around 200ml and will coat the back of the spoon. Strain through a sieve and cool until required.

# Sauces and Dressings

Most of these sauces will serve 4–6. You may have some left over, but I always think it is better to serve generous portions of sauce rather than skimpy dribbles. All the sauces need seasoning, but do this at the end after they have reduced down.

## Red Wine Sauce

*This is a classic sauce for many dishes. Perfect and very adaptable, it can be served with beef, veal, chicken and game dishes. If made with a fish stock base instead of veal it is ideal for full flavoured fish dishes too.*

Makes about 200ml

*50g chopped shallots*       *300ml Veal Stock (page 32)*
*200ml red wine*       *30g butter*

Put the shallots and red wine into a saucepan and boil until the wine is reduced by a third.

Add the veal stock and boil again, on a more gentle heat until the sauce coats the back of a spoon, around 200ml.

Strain through a fine sieve into a jug and pour back into the pan. Whisk in the butter to finish. Can be reheated gently, if necessary. Check seasoning before serving.

# Madeira Sauce

*It is worth buying a bottle of Madeira just to make this sauce. It is surprisingly versatile.*

Makes about 200ml

*1 large shallot, chopped finely*      *50g butter*
*1 clove garlic, smashed lightly but*      *120ml Madeira*
  *still whole*      *250ml Veal Stock (page 32)*

Sauté the shallot and garlic in half the butter until softened.

Add the Madeira then boil until reduced by three quarters

Pour in the stock and boil until reduced by half and the liquid is nice and glossy. Whisk in the remaining butter and strain to discard the shallots. Check the seasoning.

# Port Sauce

Serves 4–6

*50g chopped shallots*      *200 ml ruby Port*
*100g chopped mushrooms*      *300 ml Veal Stock (page 32)*
*50g fresh or frozen blackcurrants,*      *3 tablespoons double cream*
  *roughly chopped*      *Sea salt and freshly ground black*
*1 small strip orange zest*        *pepper*

Put the shallots, mushrooms, blackcurrants and orange zest into a saucepan and pour in the Port. Bring to the boil and cook until reduced by a half.

Add the veal stock and simmer until reduced down by about half again, about 25 minutes. Skim the surface with a slotted spoon if any scum forms.

Add the cream and boil for 3 minutes. Check the seasoning and serve.

# Cider Sauce

*Wonderful with pork.*

Makes about 200ml

*2 shallots, chopped finely*
*$^1/_2$ Granny Smith or Cox apple,*
  *cored and diced*
*50g butter*
*$^1/_2$ teaspoon sugar*

*2 teaspoons cider vinegar*
*200ml dry cider*
*3 tablespoons Veal Stock (page 32)*
*150ml whipping cream*
*Few drops lemon juice*

Sauté the shallots and apples in the butter until softened then sprinkle in the sugar and cook until lightly caramelised.

Add the vinegar and cook until evaporated then pour in the cider and cook until reduced down by three quarters.

Then pour in the veal stock, cook for a few moments and stir in the cream. Return to a boil then remove from the heat and stand for 10 minutes. Strain and discard the shallots and apples. Reheat the sauce gently when required, check the seasoning and add lemon juice to taste.

# Honey and Cracked Pepper Sauce

*A punchy variation of red wine sauce, perfect for duck or lamb.*

Serves 4–6

*Red Wine Sauce (page 36)*
*1 tablespoon clear honey*

*$^1/_4$ teaspoon black peppercorns,*
  *crushed*

Bring the ingredients to the boil and serve.

# Sauce Epice

*We serve this with Sesame-Crusted Scallops (page 94) but it is equally good with duck or pork.*

Serves 4

*250ml red wine vinegar*
*200g soft brown sugar*
*3 star anise*
*2 teaspoons coriander seeds*
*2 teaspoons dried pink*

*peppercorns, optional*
*2 teaspoons fennel seeds*
*Sea salt and freshly ground black*
*pepper*

Put all the ingredients into a saucepan, bring to the boil then simmer until reduced to a syrupy consistency that will cover the back of a spoon, about 150ml. Check seasoning, strain and set aside.

# Red Wine Shallots

*Cook these until they form a purée firm enough to shape into quenelles.*

Serves 4

*150g finely diced shallots*
*1 clove garlic, crushed*
*50g butter*
*200ml full bodied, deep coloured*

*red wine*
*150ml Port*
*Sea salt*

Gently sauté the shallots and garlic in the butter until softened but not coloured. Add the wine and port and simmer over a medium heat until the liquor has evaporated and you have a glossy purée of rich red shallots. Add a little salt to taste. Cool and use as required.

# Garlic Cream Sauce

Take 4–6 Garlic Confit cloves (page 25) and squeeze out the soft garlic inside. Crush with the back of a spoon and mix into a serving of the Chicken Veloute sauce (opposite). Reheat then strain through a sieve and check the seasoning.

# Chicken Veloute

*A delicate creamy sauce perfect for all light meals. By the addition of some Garlic Confit it is tranformed into the wonderfully rich Garlic Cream Sauce, opposite.*

Serves 4–6

| | |
|---|---|
| *1 large shallot, chopped* | *50g button mushrooms, sliced* |
| *100 ml white wine* | *200ml double cream* |
| *10 white peppercorns* | *Sea salt and freshly ground black* |
| *1 bay leaf* | *pepper* |
| *500 ml chicken stock (page 29)* | |

Cook the shallot in the wine with the peppercorns and bay leaf until the wine is reduced right down and the shallots softened. Add the stock and mushrooms.

Continue to simmer until reduced by half then add the cream.

Return to a simmer and cook for 5 minutes. Strain the sauce, check the seasoning and serve.

# Vermouth Veloute

*Noilly Prat is the chefs' favourite vermouth because it is dry and fragrant. Keeping a bottle of Noilly Prat in your food cupboard means you can add a rich wine flavour without having to open a bottle of wine just for a sauce.*

*Serves 4*

| | |
|---|---|
| *1 shallot, finely chopped* | *2 tablespoons double cream* |
| *1 sprig thyme* | *A pinch of paprika* |
| *$^1/_2$ bay leaf* | *60g butter, chilled and diced* |
| *100ml dry vermouth, ideally Noilly Prat* | *Sea salt and freshly ground black or white pepper* |
| *300ml fish stock (page 30)* | |

Put the shallot, thyme, bay leaf and vermouth in a saucepan and boil until reduced by a third. Pour in the fish stock and cook over a medium heat for 10 minutes, then add the cream.

Simmer the sauce until it is thick enough to coat the back of a spoon, about 200ml. Remove the thyme and bay leaf, whisk in the paprika and turn the heat down to low, making sure that the sauce does not boil.

Whisk in the butter, a little at a time, then season to taste. Spoon into a blender and whiz for about 30 seconds until thick and foamy. Serve immediately.

# Fish Vin Blanc Veloute

*A less rich sauce for fish.*

Serves 4

*1 shallot, chopped*
*$^1/_2$ bay leaf*
*100ml white wine*
*300ml Fish Stock (page 30)*
*100ml double cream*

*30g unsalted butter, cut in small*
*   cubes*
*Sea salt and freshly ground white*
*   pepper*

Place the shallots, bay leaf and white wine in a pan, boil and reduce by a third then add the stock. Bring to the boil and reduce by half or until it coats the back of a spoon.

Stir in the cream and simmer for another 5 minutes then strain through a fine sieve into another pan. Season to taste then return to a gentle simmer and whisk in the unsalted butter.


# Tapenade Sauce

*Whisk in spoonfuls of this olive and anchovy sauce into red or white wine sauce.*

Serves 4

*$^1/_2$ quantity Vermouth Veloute*
*   (page 41) or Fish Vin Blanc (above)*

*50g Tapenade (page 24)*

Heat the sauce and whisk in the Tapenade. Serve hot.

# Peppercorn Cream Sauce

*You will need green peppercorns in brine for this sauce.*

Makes about 200ml

*2 tablespoons green peppercorns in brine*
*4 shallots, chopped*
*2 cloves garlic, crushed*
*100g butter*
*¼ teaspoon cracked or coarsely*

*ground black peppercorns*
*4 tablespoons Cognac*
*120ml Madeira*
*90ml Veal Stock (page 32)*
*200ml whipping cream*
*A little fresh lemon juice*

Blanch the green peppercorns several times in plenty of boiling water. (We do it up to ten times). Drain and set aside

Gently sauté the shallots and garlic in the butter with the black peppercorns until softened, about 5 minutes then add the Cognac and flambé – i.e. carefully set alight with a match to burn off the alchohol.

Add the Madeira and cook until evaporated then add the veal stock and reduce down again.

Stir in the cream and boil a little until you have achieved a nice coating consistency. Strain and return the sauce to the pan. Mix in the green peppercorns then check for seasoning and add some lemon juice to taste.

# Pigeon Sauce

*Use the trimmings and backbones from the fresh pigeons you intend to cook.*

Serves 4

*500g fresh pigeon bones*
*2–3 tablespoons vegetable oil*
*50 ml Armagnac*
*150 ml red wine*
*450 ml Veal Stock (page 32)*

*5 juniper berries*
*Sprig fresh thyme*
*1 bay leaf*
*Sea salt and freshly ground black pepper*

Vigorously fry the pigeon bones in the oil in a large saucepan. Pour off the fat and deglaze with Armagnac until evaporated away then stir in the red wine. Boil until reduced by about a third then add the veal stock, juniper, thyme and bay.

Check the seasoning. Simmer for about 10 minutes then strain and serve hot.

# Lobster Curry Sauce

*This sauce uses Lobster Stock (page 32) and is equally delicious with all seafood and chicken. If you can't find fresh coconut then use 2 tablespoons of desiccated. See my tip below for opening a coconut.*

Serves 4 – 6

| | |
|---|---|
| 1 fresh coconut, broken open | 30g mild curry powder |
| 2 tablespoons groundnut oil | 500ml Lobster Stock (page 32) |
| 1 onion, chopped | 300ml Chicken Stock (page 29) |
| 2 shallots, chopped | 2 strips each of orange and lemon |
| 1 fat clove garlic, chopped | zest |
| 1 small stick celery, chopped | 1 large sprig fresh basil |
| 100ml dry white wine | A knob of butter |
| 5 large tomatoes, seeded and | Sea salt and freshly ground black |
| chopped | pepper |

Grate the coconut flesh on a coarse grater or whiz chunks in a strong food processor. Heat the oil in a large saucepan and gently sauté the coconut, onion, shallot, garlic and celery for about 5 minutes.

Add the wine and boil until reduced by three quarters then stir in the tomatoes and curry powder. Cook for another 5 minutes.

Pour in the two stocks, the strips of zest and basil. Bring to the boil, stirring then simmer for 20 minutes until the stocks are reduced by half. Strain through a sieve and return to the pan. Reheat, check the seasoning and whisk in the butter before serving.

## To open a coconut

Place it in a hot oven for 5 minutes. Then using a hammer, hit it hard around the middle (the equator) until it splits open. Extract the flesh with a sturdy table knife and chop.

# Caviar Sauce

*A luxurious variation on simple Fish Veloute.*

Serves 4

| | |
|---|---|
| 1 quantity of Vermouth Veloute or Fish | 20g unsalted butter |
| Vin Blanc Veloute (pages 41–42) | 50g caviar |

Reheat the sauce until hot then whisk in the butter. Remove from the heat and cool. Gently stir in the caviar as you are about to serve it so you don't damage the fragile, delicious eggs.

# Ginger Sauce (or Lemon Grass and Ginger Froth)

*Excellent with fish or lobster.*

Serves 4

100g fresh root ginger
2 shallots
1 large clove garlic
4 sticks lemon grass

100ml dry white wine
500ml Fish (page 30) or Chicken
    Stock (page 29)
150ml double cream

Peel and chop the ginger, shallots and garlic. Pull off the outer leaves of the lemon grass and chop the stems roughly. Put in a pan with the wine and boil until reduced right down then pour in the stock. Return to the boil and simmer for 10 minutes until reduced by half.

Add the cream and return to a gentle simmer for 5 more minutes. Strain through a fine sieve and serve hot. If liked, you could foam this sauce with a hand blender, i.e. Bamix.

# Red Pepper Sauce

*Good with scallops or pan-fried chicken. Piquillo peppers can be found in delis and food halls in small jars.*

Serves 4–6

2 red peppers, quartered, cored and
    chopped
200ml Chicken Stock (page 29)
5 Piquillo peppers

1 sprig each fresh thyme and basil
$1/_2$ teaspoon sugar
A good pinch sea salt

Put all ingredients in a pan bring to the boil, simmer for 10 minutes.

Remove the herbs sprigs and blitz in a blender or food processor. Strain through a fine sieve, ideally one lined with wet muslin then serve hot.

# Hollandaise Sauce

*One of the world's great sauces! A classic emulsion of eggs, vinegar and butter. Perfect with fish, chicken and vegetables. Hollandaise has to be served hot or warm and it cannot be reheated.*

Serves 6

| | |
|---|---|
| *250g butter* | *crushed* |
| *4 tablespoons cold water* | *4 egg yolks* |
| *1 tablespoon white wine vinegar* | *Juice of ¹/₂ lemon* |
| *¹/₂ teaspoon white peppercorns,* | *Sea salt* |

Clarify the butter first. Heat it slowly without stirring then carefully pour off all the golden oil leaving the milky solids behind, which should be discarded. Set aside to cool until tepid but still runny.

Combine the water, vinegar and pepper in a small, heavy based stainless steel saucepan then simmer to reduce over a low heat by a third. Set aside to cool in a heatproof bowl.

When the liquid is cold, whisk in the egg yolks and pour into a heavy based saucepan. Set over a very gentle heat and whisk continuously, making sure that the whisk comes into contact with the entire bottom surface of the pan.

Keep whisking as you slowly increase the heat; the sauce should thicken very gradually, becoming smooth and creamy after 8–10 minutes. Do not allow the temperature of the sauce to rise above 65°C (that is very hand hot) or it will curdle.

Remove the saucepan from the heat and whisking continuously, gradually blend in the cooled butter, a little at a time. Season the sauce with salt to taste.

Strain the hot sauce through a fine mesh conical sieve and serve as soon as possible, stirring in the lemon juice at the very last moment.

## Keep Hollandaise warm

Pour the sauce into a heat proof bowl set inside a pan of hot water, off the heat. Stir it occasionally to prevent a skin forming. It cannot be reheated though, so eat it in one meal.

# Mayonnaise

*Make this freshly and use the same day.*

Serves 4–6

*2 free range egg yolks*
*1 teaspoon light Dijon mustard*
*1 tablespoon white wine vinegar or*
  *fresh lemon juice plus extra to*
*taste*
*250ml groundnut or sunflower oil*
*Sea salt and freshly ground white*
  *pepper*

Whisk the yolks, mustard, vinegar or lemon juice in a large bowl with a balloon whisk until pale and thick.

Gradually whisk in the oil, starting with small drops of oil and only adding more as each lot is absorbed, increasing the drops to spoons as the mixture becomes thick and pale. If it becomes too thick then add a tablespoon of warm water to loosen it a little.

When all the oil is incorporated, check the seasoning and add more lemon juice if liked. Chill until required.

# Classic Vinaigrette

Serves 4

*1 teaspoon Dijon mustard*
*Juice of 1 lemon*
*90ml groundnut oil*
*Sea salt and freshly ground black*
  *pepper*

In a bowl, whisk together the mustard and lemon juice adding salt and pepper to taste. Whisk in the oil and use as soon as possible. If it starts to separate out, whisk again.

# Juniper Sauce

*Good with game, especially rabbit. Instead of making veal stock you could use a raw rabbit carcass after de-boning.*

Serves 4–6

*1 shallot, chopped*
*200ml red wine, preferably Côtes du Rhône*
*300ml Veal Stock (page 32) – or use rabbit bones for stock if serving with a rabbit dish*

*14 juniper berries, crushed*
*2 tablespoons  redcurrant jelly*
*40g butter, chilled and diced*
*Sea salt and freshly ground black pepper*

Put the shallot and wine in a saucepan, set over a medium heat and gently boil the wine until reduced by a third.

Add the veal stock, then the juniper berries and bubble gently for 15 minutes. Stir in the redcurrant jelly and as soon as it has been dissolved, strain the sauce through a sieve into a clean saucepan.

Return to a gentle heat and whisk in the butter, a little at a time, season to taste with salt and pepper, serve immediately.

# Hazelnut Dressing

*Lovely with quail and duck salads.*

Serves 4

*50g whole hazelnuts (skin on)*
*2 tablespoons grapeseed oil*
*1 tablespoon hazelnut oil*

*1 tablespoon balsamic vinegar*
*Sea salt and freshly ground black pepper*

Whiz everything together in a blender for a good 3–4 minutes then use as soon as possible.

# Starters

# Herb Fritters with Vegetable Crisps

*When our guests first sit at table we like to give them some nibbles of herb and vegetable crisps whilst they make their choices. The combination of fritters and colourful root crisps is very tempting.*

Serves 4–6

*1 medium raw beetroot*
*1 large parsnip*
*1 large carrot*
*(other vegetables could include*
  *butternut squash, celeriac or*
  *cassava)*
*50g picked curly parsley*
*50g mixture of picked coriander,*
  *tarragon, dill, mint or basil leaves,*
  *according to your choice*

*Groundnut or sunflower oil*
*Sea salt and freshly ground black*
  *pepper*

**Tempura Batter**
*1 egg yolk*
*150ml icecold sparkling mineral*
  *water*
*100g plain flour*

For the root vegetable crisps, peel the beetroot, parsnip and carrot then slice wafer thin on a Japanese mandolin slicer. If you have no slicer then use a swivel potato peeler.

Wash the herbs of your choice and dry in a salad spinner if you have one. Otherwise pat dry with a large clean tea towel.

Heat a deep fat fryer a third full of groundnut or sunflower oil and heat to 165°C. Deep fry the slices in small batches until crisp and slightly shrivelled. Drain on paper towel and keep warm, uncovered. Reheat the oil between batches.

For the tempura, quickly whisk together the egg yolk and water then tip in the flour all at once and whisk until just combined and the consistency of double cream. Do not over whisk.

Mix in the herbs, then heat the oil to 165°C again and drop in dessertspoonfuls and cook until crisp and bright green. Drain on paper towel and season lightly.

# King Prawn and Vegetable Tempura

*This looks like a glorious piece of abstract art on a plate! Light and crisp these are king size prawns dipped in a Japanese style vegetable batter. They can be served on their own with just a simple soy dipping sauce but for something more sophisticated try a creamy lobster sauce.*

Serves 4

1 large beetroot
1 litre Lobster Stock (page 32)
300ml double cream
Tempura batter (page 52)
12 large king prawns
1/2 small head celeriac
1 large carrot
1 medium potato, ideally Maris

Piper
1 large courgette, topped and tailed
2 teaspoons plain flour
Vegetable oil, for deep frying
A few snipped chives, to serve
Sea salt and freshly ground black
   pepper

Peel the beetroot then soak overnight in cold water and wash again until the water runs clear. Set aside.

Make the stock and boil down until reduced to around 250ml then add the cream and boil for another minute or so. Check the seasoning and set aside. Shell and de-vein the prawns, rinse and pat dry.

Peel the celeriac, carrot and potato but not the courgette. Cut the vegetables, excluding the beetroot, into very thin julienne strips either in a food processor or using a mandolin. Soak in cold water for 10 minutes then drain. Cut the beetroot separately into julienne strips and soak for 10 minutes in cold water. Pat the vegetables dry in paper towel.

Make the tempura batter and toss the prawns in the flour. When ready to serve, fill a deep fat frying pan a third deep with oil and heat to 170°C.

Quickly mix the julienne vegetables into the batter. Then coat each prawn in the vegetable batter and transfer immediately into the hot oil where they should set instantly into a pretty spiky ball. Cook in batches of 3 or 4 and reheat the oil in between.

Drain on paper towel and season lightly.

Reheat the sauce and froth with a stick blender. Divide the sauce between four warmed plates and sit 3 prawn clusters in the centre. Sprinkle with chives and serve instantly.

# Seared Foie Gras, Roast Banana and Pain D'Epice

*Although this sounds a strange combination, the actual taste of the dish is one of ingredients in perfect harmony. It has become very popular with our regular customers who keep on coming back for more! Pain d'Epice is a wonderful French spicy, honey bread that is very easy to make (see page 21).*

Serves 2

$1^1/_2$ medium size ripe bananas
2 teaspoons fresh lemon juice
1 teaspoon caster sugar
2 teaspoons crème fraiche
200g duck foie gras, sliced in two
3 tablespoons banana liqueur, e.g. Crème de banane

3 tablespoons reduced stock, preferably veal
2 slices Pain d'Epice (page 21)
Some Pain d'Epice Powder (see below)
Sea salt and freshly ground black pepper

Put the half banana in a blender with the lemon juice, sugar, crème fraiche and a good pinch of salt. Blitz until smooth and creamy. Set aside. Cut the whole banana in two.

To cook the foie gras slices, season then place in a frying pan heated to moderately hot, best side down and cook quickly until golden brown – this should take no more than 1 minute each side depending on thickness.

Cook the banana halves in the pan at the same time so they sizzle in the fat. Foie gras is perfectly cooked when it is golden brown outside, creamy inside with a core that is still a little firm. Drain the excess fat into a cup and save - see the hint below.

Stir the banana liqueur into the pan and cook for a few seconds then whisk in the stock, bubble up and strain immediately into a small jug.

Toast the Pain d'Epice. Spread with the banana purée, then add the foie gras and fried banana. Place on warm plates, pipe around the banana purée and drizzle with the sauce. Serve immediately, dusted with Pain d'Epice Powder.

## Pain d'Epice Powder

We use this to dust pan-fried foie gras. Dry out some thinly sliced Pain d'Epice in a low oven until very crispy and then crush in a food processor or blender until very fine. Rub through a fine sieve then store in a small screw topped jar.

## *Preparing Foie Gras*

Foie gras is expensive but I think worth every gram. We buy fresh duck foie gras, sold as a double lobe approximately 500–600g. Keep it chilled, but take it out of the fridge 10 minutes before cooking. We cut ours into 1cm thick slices using a knife dipped in hot water. You may need to snip out any small tubes. Don't waste trimmings – they can be used for sauces. And save the glorious golden fragrant fat that oozes out on cooking. It is sensational used for frying eggs, or tossed with some sherry vinegar for a dressing. Leftover foie gras freezes well.

# Chilled Charentais Melon Soup, Parma Ham and Basil

*Chilled melon soup might sound a strange dish but it actually works really well. It is a great summer-time dish, is always refreshing and very simple to make. I always use Charentais melon because of the wonderful flavour and lovely coloured flesh.*

Serves 2

*2 ripe Charentais melons*
*125g natural set yoghurt*
*Juice of 1 lime*
*120ml sweet white wine (e.g.*
*Sauternes or Beaumes de Venise)*
*4 slices of Parma ham*
*4 leaves of fresh basil*
*A little fine sea salt*

Peel and de-seed one of the melons, cut into large chunks and blitz in a blender or food processor to a smooth purée. Rub through a fine sieve into a bowl with the back of a ladle.

Add the yoghurt, lime juice and wine and then some salt to taste.

Chill for at least 2 hours prior to serving to enhance and maximise the flavours. When ready to serve, peel and de-seed the other melon and thinly slice, ideally on a mandolin. Arrange the slices neatly in the centre of a shallow bowl and pour around the chilled soup. Place 2 slices of Parma ham on top in slightly scrunched mounds. Shred the basil leaves and scatter on top. Serve immediately.

# Feuillete of Poached Egg with Asparagus and Hollandaise

*This dish is a combination that has been around for as long as I can remember. Poached eggs served with fresh asparagus have become a great modern day classic. Please do use the freshest free range, organic eggs you can find for the best flavour. We like to serve this with some drizzles of rich demi-glace Veal Jus (see page 33), but for vegetarians I understand this may not be suitable, so leave it out.*

Serves 4

*350g puff pastry*
*5 free range eggs, 1 separated into a yolk*
*16 asparagus spears, green or white or a combination*
*1/2 quantity Hollandaise Sauce (page 47)*
*150g butter*

*A scant 3 tablespoons white wine vinegar*
*4 teaspoons olive oil*
*4 tablespoons Veal Jus (page 33), optional*
*Sea salt and freshly ground black pepper*

The feuilletes are baked like vol-au-vents. Roll out to a 1/2cm thickness. Chill to rest for 30 minutes. Cut out 4 x 8cm discs with a pastry cutter. Heat the oven to 180°C, Gas 4.

Place the discs on a baking tray lined with baking parchment. Put 4 shallow ramekins at the corners of the tray and prop a wire rack on top. (The idea is the discs will rise up to the rack and stay evenly baked as well as taking on an attractive criss-cross top). Brush the tops with the yolk, beaten with a teaspoon of water and bake for 15 minutes. When crisp and golden, remove, cool then split each disc in half. Set aside.

Lightly peel the asparagus and trim the tough end of the stalks so that they are all the same length. Blanch in boiling salted water for 2 minutes then plunge into a basin of ice-cold water to refresh. Drain and reserve. Make the Hollandaise Sauce.

When ready to serve, melt the butter in a saucepan with 100ml water and slide in the asparagus spears and reheat gently.

Poach the eggs – bring a pan of water to a simmer, add a little salt and the white wine vinegar. Carefully crack each egg into the water and poach gently for about 3 minutes until the whites are firm and the yolks still soft. Using a slotted spoon, remove to a plate lined with paper towel to drain. Trim around the edge of the whites to neaten.

Meanwhile, reheat the asparagus in the butter and water, also reheat the Veal Jus, if using. When the eggs are poached, but the yolks are still soft, drain them and the asparagus.

To serve, place a pastry base on a plate, spoon over a little Hollandaise then add an egg and the pastry top. Place 4 reheated asparagus spears on the plate, season and trickle around the remaining Hollandaise, the Jus and dribbles of olive oil. Repeat for the next 3 plates and serve immediately.

# Tartare of Scottish Beef Bavette, Rocket Salad and Parmesan

*Tartare is a great favourite of all chefs because it uses very fresh ingredients and is quickly made. We always use bavette (or flank) of beef for this dish, not fillet, because it has a lot more flavour.*

**Serves 4**

500g *thinly sliced beef bavette*
2 *banana shallots, finely diced*
50g *capers*
1 *tablespoon Cognac*
A *few drops Tabasco or hot pepper sauce*
1 *tablespoons finely chopped parsley*

1 *teaspoon crushed sea salt flakes*
*Freshly ground black pepper*
*About 100g rocket*
A *little Classic Vinaigrette dressing (page 48)*
4 *quail egg yolks, whites discarded*
50g *Parmesan shavings*

Bat the beef with a mallet to tenderise then chop finely with a sharp knife.
Mix together with the shallot, capers, Cognac, Tabasco, parsley and seasoning.

Toss the rocket with the dressing and place on four cold plates.

Press the beef mix into 4 ring moulds, about 7cm diameter, and slide into the centre of the rocket. Make a small indent into the top and drop in a tiny yolk.

Garnish the plate with Parmesan shavings and serve lightly chilled.

# Roulade of Loch Fyne Smoked Salmon with Fromage Blanc and Avocado Coulis

*This simple dish is perfect for dinner parties as it can be prepared completely in advance. It makes a very effective starter, full of flavours in perfect union.*

Serves 4

*500g fromage blanc*
*500g long sliced smoked salmon (e.g. 30 x 12cm)*
*2 shallots, sliced thinly*
*4 tablespoons finely chopped fresh chives*
*4 tablespoons finely chopped chervil or tarragon*
*4 tablespoons finely chopped fresh parsley*

*Juice $^1/_2$ lemon*
*A little tips of salad leaves for garnish*

**Avocado Coulis**
*1 small ripe avocado*
*Juice $^1/_2$ lemon*
*1 tablespoon crème fraiche*
*Sea salt and freshly ground black pepper*

Spoon the fromage blanc into a large piece of muslin and either twist and hang up like a bag on a hook or place in a sieve over a bowl. Leave overnight or about 12 hours in the fridge to drain then discard the milky fluids.

In the meantime, select four long slices of salmon about 30 x 12 cm and trim to neaten. Chop the remaining trimmings very finely.

Mix the drained fromage blanc with the shallots, herbs, salmon trimmings and juice of half the lemon and add seasoning to taste. When smooth spoon into a piping bag fitted with a plain 1cm wide nozzle.

Cover a work surface with a sheet of Clingfilm about two to three times the size of the salmon slices. Lay a salmon slice along one edge towards you making sure there are no gaps, breaks or tears.

Pipe a quarter of the filling along the bottom edge, and then roll up tightly in the salmon. Overwrap in the Clingfilm, twisting the ends to make the roulade tight.

Repeat with the other 3 salmon slices and filling, so you have four tightly rolled salmon roulades. Chill again.

Make the avocado coulis. Peel and blitz the avocado in a food processor until very smooth beating in lemon juice, crème fraiche and seasoning.

To serve, unroll the roulades onto plates and trim off the ends to neaten. Serve topped with some salad leaf tips and pipe avocado coulis alongside.

# Cep & Potato Risotto

*Risotto is a very popular starter or main course in Simpsons and is always a great test of the cook's ability. The secret is to use a good quality Italian rice, such as Vialone Nano or Arborio and to stir the grains vigorously during the cooking process to help the starch form that lovely velvety sauce associated with the very best risottos. The variety of risotto is endless; this is a great one for the autumn and winter season.*

### Serves 4

*90g butter*
*1 large shallot, finely chopped*
*250g fresh ceps, chopped*
*200g risotto rice, e.g. Vialone Nano
    or Arborio*
*100ml white wine*
*900ml Vegetable Stock (page 33),
    heated until boiling*
*100g potato, diced and lightly
    cooked*
*2 tablespoons Mascarpone*

*60g freshly grated Parmesan cheese*
*Sea salt and freshly ground black
    pepper*

**To serve**
*Parmesan Tuiles, (page 24), or
    25g shavings of Parmesan cheese*
*4 tablespoons Veal Jus (page 33),
    optional*
*3 tablespoons Cep or truffle oil*
*Sprigs fresh parsley*

Heat 30g of the butter in a medium size saucepan and add the shallots and ceps. Cook gently for 2–3 minutes then stir in the rice and cook for a minute or so until opaque.

Add the wine and cook until completely absorbed. Gradually add the stock to the rice, stirring vigorously, this should take at least 15 minutes until the rice is al dente, with a slight bite in the centre.

Add the rest of the butter, the cooked potatoes, Mascarpone and half the grated Parmesan. Season and serve on a warmed plate garnished with the Parmesan Tuiles or shavings, drizzled with jus, if using, and olive oil and topped with remaining grated cheese and parsley sprigs.

# Broccoli Risotto

*A light risotto, popular in summer and spring.*

Serves 4

90g butter
1 large shallot, chopped finely
200g rice
100ml white wine
900ml Vegetable Stock (page 33)
250g broccoli florets, stalks cut
   away, florets trimmed very small

2 tablespoons Mascarpone cheese
60g grated fresh Parmesan plus
   some shavings to serve
100ml Veal Jus (page 33), optional
A little olive oil, to drizzle
Sea salt and freshly ground black
   pepper

Make the risotto in the same way as the Cep & Potato Risotto (page 70). Place half the butter in a small pan, add the shallot, cook gently without colour for 2 to 3 minutes then add the rice.

Stir in the wine and cook until reduced right down and then gradually add the stock stirring vigorously. This whole process should take about 15 minutes until the rice has a slight bite in the middle.

Meanwhile, blanch the florets in some salted water for about 2 minutes then drain. At this point finish the risotto with the remaining butter to give it a rich texture, add the Mascarpone cheese, grated Parmesan and half the florets of pre-cooked broccoli. Check the seasoning.

Serve topped with the remaining broccoli and shavings of Parmesan with the Veal Jus, if using, and olive oil drizzled around.

# Deep-Fried Haloumi Cheese with Tomato & Onion Salad and Capers

*This dish takes me back to my childhood. A typical Mediterranean dish full of flavours using very basic ingredients. I always want to use Greek olive oil with this dish, then add capers at the end just to cut through the richness of a fresh pressed quality olive oil. This is a great summer dish but can be eaten all year round. Haloumi, a firm pressed cheese, is only made in Cyprus, but is widely available in various delis and is stocked by most supermarket chains. It cooks wonderfully well.*

Serves 4

*1 Haloumi cheese, about 250g*
*4 large plum tomatoes*
*2 spring onions, finely diced*
*3 tablespoons finely chopped chives*
*3 tablespoons finely chopped flat leaf parsley*
*1 tablespoon baby capers*
*150ml extra virgin olive oil,*

*preferably lovely fruity Greek oil*
*3 tablespoons white wine vinegar or fresh lemon juice*
*Vegetable oil, for deep frying*
*A few tips of salad leaves, to garnish*
*Sea salt and freshly ground black pepper*

Cut the Haloumi into finger sized pieces and pat dry on paper towel.

Wash and slice the tomatoes, and arrange in overlapping circles on two plates.

For the dressing, mix together the onion, chives, parsley and capers with the oil, adding vinegar or lemon juice according to choice and seasoning to taste. (Personally I think lemon juice works better with this recipe). Spoon over the tomatoes.

Heat oil in a deep fryer to 175°C and fry the cheese for about 2 minutes until nicely golden. Drain on paper towel again and stack on top of the tomatoes. If you wish you could garnish with some salad leaf tips.

# Tomato, Courgette and Aubergine Tart with Parmesan Herb Salad

*This is a great vegetarian starter, which can also be used as a main course. It's full of the flavours of the south of France and can be enhanced with the use of Pesto (page 23) or Tapenade (page 24).*

### Serves 4

1 quantity Aubergine Caviar (page 23)
200g puff pastry
8 large plum tomatoes, sliced thinly
2 medium courgettes, sliced very thinly
A little olive oil, for brushing
80g Parmesan cheese shavings
Small handful picked chervil leaves
Small handful picked tarragon
leaves
2 tablespoons chopped fresh chives
About 150g mixed salad leaves
  including rocket, frisée, baby red
  chard, etc.
A little Classic Vinaigrette (page 48)
Sea salt and freshly ground black
  pepper

Make up a batch of Aubergine Caviar and set aside.

Roll out the pastry to a rectangle about 2mm thick (the thickness of a £1 coin). Prick and place on a non-stick baking sheet. Lay a sheet of non-stick baking parchment on top then another baking sheet. Heat the oven to 160°C and bake the pastry for 20 minutes or until golden brown.

When the pastry is cooled, cut out the tart bases, approximately 10–12cm in diameter using a small saucer as a template. Allow to cool completely.

Spread the bases with some of the aubergine mix and then layer on the tomato and courgette slices in rings. Brush with a little oil to coat. Season and return to the oven for 7–8 minutes until piping hot.

Remove and top with the Parmesan slices and return to the oven until they just melt.

Meanwhile, toss the herbs and salad leaves with some vinaigrette and divide between four plates, then place a tart on top of each. Spoon some more Aubergine Caviar on top. We shape ours into neat quenelles using two dessertspoons. Serve freshly baked.

# Crab Torte

*A dish in perfect harmony; all the ingredients marry happily together and look very pretty on the plate. Use a freshly cooked crab, thereby encouraging your diners to think that they are on the seashore surrounded by the smell of the ocean!*

Serves 4

*80g puff pastry*
*200g smoked salmon, diced finely*
*200g fresh white crab meat*
*2 tablespoons fresh Mayonnaise*
  *(page 48)*
*1 lemon*
*Creamed Guacamole (below)*

**To serve**
*Red Pepper Essence (opposite)*
*A little mixed salad leaf tips*
*4 Sesame Tuiles (page 24), to serve*
*A little paprika, to dust*
*Sea salt and freshly ground white*
  *pepper*

Roll out the pastry to a rectangle about 2mm thick (the thickness of a £1 coin). Prick and place on a non-stick baking sheet. Lay a sheet of non-stick baking parchment on top then another baking sheet. Heat the oven to 160°C and bake the pastry for 20 minutes or until golden brown.

Take a metal ring mould, 5–6cm diameter and cut out four round discs. Place the discs on a flat plate and fix the metal rings on top (they should be about 5–6 cm deep).

Press the diced salmon firmly down on top of the pastry discs using the back of a teaspoon.

Mix the crab meat with enough Mayonnaise to bind then add lemon juice to taste and seasoning. Spoon this on top of the salmon, pressing down again with the spoon. Chill until ready to serve.

When ready to serve, make up the guacamole and spoon on top of the crab then lift each torte onto a serving plate using a palette knife and lift off the ring mould. Garnish with some salad leaves on top plus the Sesame Tuiles and Red Pepper Essence squeezed into little dollops. Dust on fine lines of paprika, if liked.

## Creamed Guacomole

*2 teaspoons finely chopped shallot*
*1 teaspoon finely chopped fresh red*
  *chilli*
*1 ripe avocado, preferably Hass*

*Juice ¹/₂ lime*
*1 teaspoon Mascarpone*
*Sea salt and freshly ground black*
  *pepper*

Put the chopped shallot and chilli in a sieve and rinse well under cold water. Pat dry.

Halve the avocado, stone and scoop the flesh into a bowl, roughly mashing with a fork. Add the rest of the ingredients then fold together. Use immediately.

## Red Pepper Essence

*2 red peppers, cored, seeded and*     *A little potato flour*
  *chopped*

Blitz the peppers to a smooth juicy purée then rub through a seive into a saucepan.
Discard the pulp.

Boil the juice until reduced by a third.

Slake about $\frac{1}{2}$ teaspoon of potato flour with a little cold water and mix in, stirring
until thickened. Cool and pour into a squeezy bottle.

# Orzo with Crab, Chilli and Pesto

*Orzo are tiny rice shaped pasta, hence the name which is Italian for rice. They are very popular in Italy and make delightful salads, like this one, perfect as a starter for a chic, yet casual meal. I always like to double check white crab meat for any stray chips of shell using the tip of a fork.*

Serves 4

*250g Orzo pasta*
*1 large mild red chilli, seeded and finely sliced*
*A knob of butter*
*3–4 tablespoons Gremolata (page 22)*
*300g picked white crab meat*

*100g wild rocket leaves, roughly torn*
*Shavings of fresh Parmesan*
*Sea salt and freshly ground black pepper*

Cook the Orzo in boiling, salted water according to pack instructions, about 12 minutes. Drain and set aside.

Cook the chilli lightly in the butter in a medium saucepan for a minute or two until just softened then mix in the Gremolata. Then stir in the Orzo and fork in the crab. Reheat until piping hot and check the seasoning and stir in the torn rocket leaves.

Divide between four warmed bowls and serve immediately, topped with Parmesan shavings.

# Beetroot Carpaccio and Dressing

*Equally delicious on it's own as either a salad or a starter.*

Serves 4

500g medium sized beetroots
3 tablespoons olive oil
1 tablespoon cider vinegar
1 teaspoon fine sea salt

1 teaspoon sugar
1 tablespoon finely chopped fresh
  parsley
Freshly ground black pepper

Cook 250g of the beetroot until just tender, then cool and peel. Peel the raw beetroot and grate coarsely. (You may also like to protect your hands with rubber gloves so they won't stain!)

Slice the cooked beetroot very thinly on a mandolin, into a shallow dish. Mix together the oil, vinegar, salt and pepper to taste then pour over the beetroot and mix in well. Cover and leave for at least 4 hours or overnight, then drain off, and save the excess juices.

Meanwhile, make the dressing. Place the raw grated beetroot in a saucepan with the sugar adding just enough water to cover. Boil gently for about 10 minutes then strain off and reserve the juice, pressing through a sieve. Return the juice to a pan together with the marinating juices and boil down to a syrupy glaze. Cool and mix in the chopped parsley.

Serve the beetroot in overlapping slices with the dressing and some olive oil drizzled around.

# Fish and Shellfish

# Cod with Lentils and Garlic Cream Sauce

*A classic combination – chunky cod served with little lentils is not only delicious but very healthy! Choose the little blue-green Puy lentils from France, or failing that the Canadian lentilles verts.*

Serves 4

*100g lentils de Puy*
*2 carrots, finely chopped*
*2 sticks celery, finely chopped*
*1 onion*
*1 clove garlic, lightly crushed*
*1 sprig fresh thyme*
*1 shallot*
*4 x 180g cod fillets, thick cut and*
  *skin on*
*A little flour for dusting*
*A little olive oil, for frying*

*About 40g butter*
*About 150g baby leaf spinach*
*Sea salt and freshly ground black*
  *pepper*

**To serve**
*Garlic Cream Sauce (page 40)*
*Some Garlic Confits (page 25)*
*A few flat leaf parsley leaves,*
  *shredded*

First, prepare the Garlic Cream Sauce and Garlic Confits.

Cook the lentils. Place them in a pan and cover with cold water. Roughly chop one carrot, one celery stick and the onion and add to the pan with the garlic and thyme. Bring to the boil then simmer gently for around 15 minutes until tender and the water absorbed. Remove the vegetables and thyme, season to taste and set aside.

Finely chop the remaining carrot, celery and shallot. Boil gently in some salted water until tender. Drain and mix with the lentils.

When ready to cook, heat the oven to 190°C, Gas 5. Coat the cod in flour and shake off excess. Heat some oil in a large oven proof frying pan (e.g. cast iron) and fry the fish, skin side down for about 2 minutes.

Add knobs of half the amount of butter to the pan and melt. Carefully flip over the fish and baste with the juices. Season and place in the oven for 4–5 minutes until the top is just firm. Remove from the oven and allow to rest, then remove the skin.

Add the remaining butter to a saucepan and toss in the spinach, stirring until just wilted. Season and drain on paper towel.

To serve, reheat the lentils and mix with the spinach. Spoon into the centre of four warmed plates, top with the cod and scatter with shredded parsley.

Heat the sauce and spoon around and serve with some Garlic Confits alongside.

# Curried Monkfish with Gremolata Chick Peas

*With its slightly sweet flesh and firm texture, monkfish is delicious rolled in mild curry spices and then pan-fried. We like to serve it with chick peas tossed with parsley, lemon and garlic gremolata and serve with chard, although you could use large leaf spinach instead. Try and buy long thinner monkfish tails, about 750g in weight as they look more elegant on a plate.*

Serves 4

*2 tails of monkfish, about 750g each, skinned and trimmed*
*1 tablespoon mild curry powder*
*3 tablespoons plain flour*
*4 tablespoons Gremolata (page 22)*
*1 bunch Swiss chard*

*A good knob of butter*
*200g cooked or canned chick peas*
*A little olive oil*
*Some lemon oil, to drizzle*
*Sea salt and freshly ground black pepper*

Slit each monkfish tail in half and trim to 4 neat loins. Make sure all the grey membrane is removed from the monkfish fillets to ensure they cook flat and don't curl up. Mix together the curry powder, flour and some salt. Toss the monkfish in the flour, shake off the excess and then set aside.

Make the Gremolata and set aside. Cut the leaves from the stems of the chard. Slice the stems into 2cm pieces and cook in just enough salted water to cover, for about 5 minutes until tender. Drain. Sauté the leaves in some butter for about 3 minutes then season.

To cook the fish, preheat the oven to 180°C, Gas 4. Heat an ovenproof frying pan (e.g. cast iron) with a tablespoon of oil. Place the monkfish in the pan and cook on all sides until golden brown and sealed. Season well and place in the oven for about for 8 minutes until just cooked. Then remove and rest for 5 minutes.

Mix the chick peas in with the chard leaves and the Gremolata and heat well. Divide between four warmed plates and top with the fish. Scatter around the chard stems and drizzle with a little lemon oil. Serve immediately.

# John Dory with Tomato Tart and Tapenade Sauce

*John Dory is a fish that deserves more popularity, especially as it is fished in British waters. It is the only fish that has fillets which divide into 3 parts and we present it divided as such on a plate. In this Mediterranean style recipe the John Dory is served with a light vegetable tart.*

Serves 4

$^1/_2$ quantity Tapenade (page 24)
150ml Fish Veloute (page 42), made
  with red wine
4 x 120g fillets of John Dory, skinned
A little olive oil, for frying
150g baby leaf spinach
A knob of butter
Sea salt and freshly ground black
  pepper

**For the tarts**
100g puff pastry
1 medium courgette
4 plum tomatoes
4 large basil leaves, fried until crisp
4 shavings of Parmesan cheese

Make the Tapenade and Fish Veloute and set aside.

For the tarts, roll out the pastry to the thickness of a £1 coin then cut into 4 rectangles about 12 x 6cm. Prick the pastry and set aside whilst you heat the oven to 200°C, Gas 6.

Place the pastry on a heavy baking sheet lined with baking parchment, top with more parchment and another baking sheet. Bake flat for about 10 minutes until golden brown. Remove the top baking tray and paper. Spread the pastry with Tapenade.

Slice the courgettes and tomatoes thinly and evenly and arrange alternately on the puff pastry rectangles. Return to the oven for 5 – 8 minutes. Remove from oven and season, then brush with olive oil and lay a basil leaf and the Parmesan shavings on top. Return to the oven until the cheese has melted. Keep warm whilst you cook the fish.

Heat some oil in a non-stick frying pan. Season the fish and cook for about 2 minutes each side until golden brown. Set aside for a few minutes.

Sauté the spinach in a little butter until wilted. Season and drain on paper towel. Divide between four warmed plates and put the fillets on top. Spoon around small dabs of Tapenade and serve immediately with the tarts.

# Lemon Sole with Courgettes, Carrots, Melon and a Ginger Sauce

*We have a way of cooking sole fillets that are still attached to the central bone so that they cook flat. You will need a razor sharp filleting knife for this. Alternatively, you can cook the fillets completely detached though the serving won't be as impressive. We have an unusual accompaniment of melon and lettuce with this dish, it works well – try it and see! The picture shows a courgette flower fritter which is an optional garnish.*

Serves 4

*4 whole lemon soles, about
  650–700g each, skinned
1 quantity Ginger Sauce (page 46)
1 Charentais melon
2 carrots, peeled
1 medium courgette, topped and*

*  tailed
2 large leaves Little Gem lettuce
A little olive oil, for frying
50g butter
Sea salt and freshly ground black
  pepper*

If you can't skin whole soles yourself, ask the fishmonger but make sure they are still left on the bone. Cut off the heads and tails but leave on the outside 'frills'. Then insert the tip of a sharp filleting knife at the sides and work your way towards the central bone cutting along the rib bones until you get to the centre spine bone of the fish. You will need to do this 4 times to release all 4 fillets from their bones then fold the fillets back and cut out the fillet bones with sharp scissors. When this is complete, you will be left with four sole fillets still attached to the centre spine bone. Set aside.

Make the Ginger Sauce and set aside. Peel the melon and cut into desired shapes. We use an oval shaped Parisienne scoop but you can use a melon baller or just cut the melon into segments if you prefer.

Halve the carrots and courgette lengthways then slice on a mandolin or Japanese slicer into thin ribbons.

Meanwhile, pan fry the sole over a medium heat in a non-stick frying pan with a tablespoon of oil for 3–4 minutes each side until cooked then remove from the heat. Add a knob of butter to the pan towards the end and baste over the fish. Season, remove from the heat and rest.

Warm the melon in a small pan under the grill or in the microwave.

Bring a large pan of salted water to the boil. Blanch the carrot slices for $1\frac{1}{2}$ minutes then add the courgettes and lettuce leaves until just wilted. Drain and toss with the remaining butter until well-coated.

Reheat the sauce gently. Serve the sole topped with the courgette, carrot and lettuce. Spoon the sauce around and position the melon as in the photograph opposite. Season and serve.

# Pave of Salmon with Fennel and Artichoke Barigoule with its own Nage

*A pave of salmon is an evenly cut fillet, like a pavement slab, hence the name. We serve it nestled on a wonderful bed of braised artichoke and fennel and make a light sauce with the pan juices. Little carrot slices and petit pois give it a delightful summery look. In the restaurant we serve this with a garnish of trimmed baby artichoke and a Parmesan wafer.*

Serves 4

*4 x 150g middle cut fillets of salmon, skinned*
*A little olive oil*
*A large knob of butter plus 125g for sauce*
*4 small artichokes, prepared*
*1 small carrot*
*Some petit pois, to serve*
*Sea salt and freshly ground black pepper*

**For the Barigoule**
*1 large globe artichoke*
*A squeeze of lemon juice*
*2 bulbs of fennel*
*1 onion, finely sliced*
*1 carrot, finely sliced*
*2 tablespoons fennel seeds*
*1 tablespoon pink peppercorns*
*3 star anise*
*1 tablespoon coriander seeds*
*300ml Chicken Stock (page 29)*

Prepare the Barigoule. Start with the globe artichoke. First, break off the stalk and peel off the tough outer leaves until you see the cream and purple inner leaves. Trim around the base of the artichoke with a small knife to remove all the remaining leaves. With a large knife, cut off the fine fibres from the centre of the artichoke then, using a spoon, scoop out the fibrous choke leaving just the firm base which can then be cut into wedges and placed in lemon water.

For the fennel, first trim off the stalks and peel the outer layers if tough, otherwise run a vegetable peeler down the outside to remove the ribs. Place the fennel bulb upright on a board and cut in half. Remove the core from each half in a neat 'V' shape with a sharp knife. Slice the fennel half into fine strips across the grain. Crush the whole spices in a pestle and mortar and tie in a muslin cloth.

In a saucepan, gently sweat the onion in some olive oil for 5 minutes then add the fennel and cook until softened, about 5 minutes. Add the chicken stock, 1 sliced carrot, artichoke and muslin bag. Bring to the boil, cover and simmer for 20–25 minutes until tender. Remove from the heat and cool with the spice bag to infuse, then remove the bag.

Strain the Barigoule juices into a small saucepan and bring to the boil. Whisk in the 125g butter slowly to create a light buttery sauce, termed a Nage. Season with salt and pepper and keep warm. Boil the small artichokes until just tender, drain upside down then toss in a little butter and keep warm.

Boil the small artichokes until just tender, drain upside down, then toss in a little butter and keep warm.

Peel the remaining small carrot and make 4 grooves down the sides with a cannelling tool – then slice thinly into little daisy shapes. Blanch in some water then toss with a little butter. Blanch the petit pois and toss with a little butter.

When ready to serve, season the salmon on both sides and pan fry in olive oil in a non-stick frying pan for about 3–4 minutes on a medium heat. Then turn over and cook for 2–3 minutes, taking care not to over cook. Season again.

Reheat the Barigoule, check the seasoning and spoon the vegetables onto four warmed plates. Top with the salmon fillets, scatter around the carrots and petit pois, add the small artichokes and spoon over the light nage.

# Pave of Salmon with Potato 'Scales' and Caviar Sauce

*This is a dish more suited to a formal dining occasion. The fish is topped with thin sliced potato and the sauce has sevruga caviar stirred in for the ultimate luxurious treat. For a cheaper alternative use the farmed avruga caviar.*

**Serves 4**

150g butter plus extra to serve
1 quantity Fish Vin Blanc Veloute
   sauce (page 42)
4 x 150g salmon fillets, skinned
1 tablespoon potato flour or
   cornflour
Approx. 16 waxy potatoes, ideally

Ratte potatoes or Charlotte
A little olive oil, for frying
250g baby leaf spinach
50g caviar, ideally sevruga
Sea salt and freshly ground black
   pepper

Make clarified butter by melting 100g of the solid butter and then pouring off the golden oil. Keep warm.

Make the sauce and keep warm. Take care not to add too much salt at this stage to allow for the addition of the salty caviar later.

Coat the salmon fillets on one side with the potato flour and place on a tray with the floured side uppermost. Slice the potatoes lengthways approx. 2mm thick. For best results use a mandolin.

From the slices, cut tiny discs using a small pastry cutter or an apple corer, 1–1.5 cm in diameter is ideal. When you have enough slices lay them in overlapping rows on the salmon, starting at one end and working your way to the other.

When all four portions have been covered in 'scales', brush each with clarified butter to seal the potatoes and chill until ready to cook.

Heat a non-stick pan large enough to take the four salmon fillets and place the salmon in the pan, potato side down. Cook over a moderate heat, about 5 minutes, to give a really crisp finish to the potato layer.

Meanwhile, heat the remaining 50g butter in a pan, when it begins to sizzle add the baby spinach and cook until the spinach has wilted. Season to taste and drain well on paper towel

Turn the fish carefully in the pan to cook the other underside for about 2 more minutes. Season the potato top lightly.

Place a little spinach in the centre of 4 warmed plates and place a salmon and potato pave on top. Reheat the sauce and stir in the caviar then pour the sauce around the spinach and serve immediately.

# Skate Wings with Tomato, Cucumber & Grain Mustard Sauce

*This stunning dish is actually quite easy to make. You will need 4 large thick fillets of skate and some white wine sauce. Skate is a cartilaginous fish and as such has no little bones so it is very easy to eat.*

**Serves 4**

$^1/_2$ quantity Fish Vin Blanc Veloute
   sauce (page 42)
3 large plum tomatoes
$^1/_2$ cucumber
4 x 180g skate wings
A little flour, for dusting
150ml Veal Jus (page 33)
4 tablespoons red wine

Olive oil, for frying
75g butter
150g baby leaf spinach
1 tablespoon coarse grain mustard,
   ideally Pommery
Sea salt and freshly ground black
   pepper

Make up the Fish Vin Blanc Veloute sauce and set aside.

Briefly dip the tomatoes in boiling water, remove with a slotted spoon to a bowl of iced water then slip off the skins. Halve, scoop out the seeds and chop the flesh into 1cm neat dice. Peel the cucumber with a swivel vegetable peeler and scoop out balls of cucumber using a small melon baller, or cut into neat cubes.

Boil the wine until reduced to a tablespoon then add the Veal Jus. Set aside.

Dust the fish with flour, shaking off excess. Heat some olive oil in a large frying pan and cook the fish, presentation side down first, for about 2 minutes over a moderate heat until golden brown, slide in a knob of the butter,  season in the pan then carefully turn over and cook the other side. Slide the fish onto a plate and set aside to rest.

In a separate pan, heat half the remaining butter and gently sauté the cucumber balls and tomato dice for 1–2 minutes until softened but still crunchy. Season and set aside.

Sauté the spinach in the remaining butter until just wilted. Season also. Divide between warmed plates and put a skate wing on top.

Reheat the sauce and whisk in the mustard. Scatter around the tomato and cucumber and drizzle the red wine jus around. Serve hot.

# Sesame-Crusted Scallops with Chicory Marmalade

*This dish is a marriage of the cuisines of East and West. But, as with all fusion food, you must ensure that the flavours work well together rather than battling in opposition. I think this dish is in perfect harmony. You will need some Sauce Epice and Chicory Marmalade.*

Serves 4

*Sauce Epice (page 40)*
*Chicory Marmalade (page 25)*
*12 extra large fresh scallops*
*1 egg white, lightly beaten*
*50g sesame seeds*
*A little vegetable oil for frying*

*12 large leaves chicory*
*Some slices Lemon Confit (page 26)*
*Some lemon oil*
*Sea salt and freshly ground black*
*  pepper*

Make the Sauce Epice and Chicory Marmalade then set aside.

Prepare the scallops by pulling out the black intestine cord and the small hard side muscle. (The corals/roes can be saved and dried until brittle for coral powder – page 105).

Lightly beat the egg white on a small plate and press one side of the scallops in it. Put the sesame seeds onto another small flat plate and press on the egg washed scallops ensuring they have a nice even coating on top. Set aside, seed side down.

Heat a large non-stick frying pan with a thin layer of oil and add the scallops, sesame crust side first. Cook for 2 minutes on a moderate heat, ensuring they do not over brown, then flip them carefully over and cook for a further 1 minute. Remove from the heat.

Reheat the Chicory Marmalade and spoon onto the centre of four warmed plates. Fix 3 chicory leaves on top, then 3 scallops each on the leaves. Drizzle over a little lemon oil and fix a Lemon Confit slice in the middle. Spoon around the Epice Sauce and a little more oil. Serve hot.

# Carpaccio of Tuna with Cucumber and White Radish Salad and Wasabi Mayonnaise

*This light dish has a Japanese twist. Make sure to buy the tuna from a reputable fishmonger as it should be very fresh. Wasabi is a type of horseradish, sold in tubes. It is quite fiery so use cautiously.*

Serves 4

350g fresh tuna fillet
2 teaspoons coarsely ground black pepper
4 teaspoons Maldon salt plus extra for sprinkling
A little olive oil
$^1/_2$ cucumber
$^1/_2$ large mooli
1 spring onion
2 teaspoons finely chopped red

pepper
A little lemon or extra virgin olive oil
A little rice wine vinegar
Squeeze fresh lemon juice
2 tablespoons Mayonnaise (page 48)
Wasabi paste, to taste
A few pea shots or other salad leaves, e.g, cress or lamb lettuce

Trim the tuna fillet into a roll. Cut any trimmings into small dice and chill.

Heat a heavy non-stick frying pan until hot. Sprinkle the pepper and salt onto a dinner plate and roll the tuna in it. Add a little oil to the hot pan and immediately sear the tuna in the hot pan, turning to cook evenly. This should take seconds and the insides remain raw. Remove and cool, then wrap in Clingfilm and chill.

Cut the cucumber and mooli into slices 1 x 6cm, then layer in a colander sprinkling lightly with more salt in between the layers. Leave to drain for 15 minutes.

Remove 4 strips each of cucumber and mooli and cut into fine dice. Finely chop the spring onion and mix with the diced tuna, chopped red pepper, a little lemon or olive oil, vinegar, lemon juice and seasoning to taste. Set aside and chill.

Mix a small dab of wasabi paste into the Mayonnaise and taste. If you want a stronger flavour, then add more.

When ready to serve, unwrap the tuna and cut into 12–16 slices. Brush each slice with a little lemon or olive oil and place, overlapping, on 4 plates. Divide the diced salad, remaining cucumber and mooli slices and wasabi mayo between the plates, garnish with the pea shoots or leaves and serve.

# Pan-Fried Turbot with Spinach and Goats' Cheese, Broccoli Purée and Chorizo Foam

Serves 4

2 heads broccoli
125g butter (75g plus 50g)
12 slices mature chorizo
A little olive oil, for frying
4 x 150g fillets of turbot
A little flour for dusting
500g baby leaf spinach, picked, stalks trimmed and washed
100g semi-soft goats' cheese,
crumbled
Sea salt and freshly ground black pepper

**Chorizo foam**
500ml Chicken Stock (page 29)
75g raw chorizo, diced
5 tablespoons double cream

Make the chorizo foam first. Gently simmer the stock and chorizo for 15 minutes, making sure it does not reduce too much. Top up with water if it does evaporate. Add the cream, return to a gentle boil then strain into a high sided saucepan and keep warm.

Make the broccoli purée. Trim the florets and cook in fast boiling salted water until tender, about 5 minutes. Drain and blend to a velvety smooth purée with 75g of the butter. Season and set aside.

Heat a grill and cook the chorizo slices briefly until they crisp.

Heat a large non-stick frying pan with a thin film of oil. Dust the fish quickly with flour and shake off any excess. Shallow fry the fish for about 2 minutes each side until just firm. Do not over cook. Remove to a plate, season lightly and keep warm.

Toss the spinach into the pan with the 50g of butter and stir fry until wilted. Season and drain and then mix with the goats' cheese. Divide the spinach between four warmed plates and spoon the broccoli purée alongside. Put the turbot on the spinach and arrange the chorizo alongside.

Reheat the chorizo foam and froth with a stick blender and spoon onto the plates. Serve immediately.

# Sea Bass with Lobster Noodles and Lobster Sauce

*Sea bass is one of the finest fish for eating so we like to do it justice and serve it with homemade lobster flavoured noodles and a beautiful Lobster Sauce (page 56). To make the noodles, you will need the coral of fresh lobster, also known as tomalley. When making the pasta, do not be alarmed by the colour of the raw paste, as soon as you cook the pasta in boiling water it changes to a beautiful coral colour. You will also find a pasta rolling machine helpful for this recipe.*

Serves 4

*Lobster Noodles (see opposite)*
*Lobster Sauce (page 54)*
*Olive oil, for frying*
*4 x 150g fillets sea bass, skin on*
*A little fresh lemon juice*
*2 heads bok choi*

*A little butter, to serve*
*Coral Powder (see opposite), or a*
  *little paprika for dusting*
*Sea salt and freshly ground black*
  *pepper*

Make the pasta for the noodles first. You only need half these noodles for 4 servings, so freeze the rest for another time. They can be cooked from frozen.

Make the Lobster Sauce and set aside.

When ready to serve, heat about a tablespoon of oil in a large non-stick frying pan and fry the bass skin side down for about 3–4 minutes. You will see the flesh changing colour as it cooks. When the flesh looks three quarters cooked, season the flesh and add lemon juice then turn it over carefully to complete the cooking on the flesh side. Set aside to rest.

Trim the base of the bok choi and then boil in a large pan of salted water for around 2 minutes. Drain well and toss with some butter and seasoning. Keep warm.

Cook the noodles in a large pan of boiling, salted water until pink and cooked thoroughly, about 4 minutes. Drain and return to the pan with a knob of butter and a spoonful of lobster sauce.

Divide into four and place on four warmed plates. (In the restaurant we wrap noodles around a large fork to make a tower, it's a neat technique).

When you are ready to serve, lay out bok choi leaves on the plates and sit a sea bass fillet on top. Heat and whisk the remaining sauce to a froth with a hand held stick blender. Spoon the sauce around the plate and serve lightly dusted with paprika or Coral Powder.

## To Make Scallop Coral Powder

Use the orange roes removed from fresh scallops. Freeze until you have at least 8–12 roes. Lay them out on a baking tray lined with silicone baking sheets. Dry out for around 24 hours in a low oven, even overnight, until the roes are so brittle they snap. Break into several pieces then grind down in a powerful blender to a fine powder. Store in a screw-topped jar and use as required.

## Lobster Noodles

*4 free range eggs*
*2 egg yolks*
*90g lobster coral (or as much as you*
*  can gather – it does freeze)*

*550g pasta '00' flour or fine*
*  semolina*
*1 tablespoon olive oil*
*1 teaspoon fine sea salt*

You will find this makes enough noodles for 8 servings but the remainder can be frozen. Whiz together the eggs, yolks and lobster coral then rub through a fine sieve into a bowl.

Place the flour, oil, salt and coral mixture into a food processor and process until the mixture resembles moist breadcrumbs.

Tip the mixture onto a clean worktop and knead together with your hands to a smooth, slightly soft dough. Wrap the dough in Clingfilm and chill for 30 minutes.

To make noodles, break off egg sized pieces of dough and feed through the rollers several times starting on a thick setting, and gradually turning the dial to the last but one thin setting.

Pass the dough sheets through a noodle cutting attachment on the machine, sprinkling with semolina as you roll, and leave to dry flat on a tray lined with a clean tea towel. If you don't have a pasta machine, you can roll out the dough using a rolling pin and cut the noodles by hand, but a machine makes the job much easier!

# Tronconnettes of Lobster, Lobster Noodles, Lobster Froth

*Our lobsters come from Scotland, where the pure, clear cold waters give the lobster flesh a fine flavour. Allow one lobster (approximately 600–700g each) per head for a main course or for 2 starter portions. Fresh lobster heads and shells can be used to make Lobster Sauce and the lobster corals for pasta, so that every piece of this exquisite shellfish is used.*

Serves 4

*4 x 600–700g native lobsters, prepared into tronconnettes see page below*
*500ml Lobster Stock (page 32)*
*100ml double cream*

*Lobster noodles (page 101)*
*A knob of butter*
*Olive oil, for brushing*
*Juice 1 lemon*
*Leaves of flat leaf parsley*

## How to Prepare Fresh Lobster for Tronconnettes

Kill the lobsters by inserting a heavy knife into the cross on top of the head between the eyes. Remove heads. These can be washed and used for making the Lobster Stock.

Twist off the large and smaller lobster claws. The large front claws have a lot of meat in them.

Take the lobster body tails and push a metal skewer down the back between the shell and the flesh. This keeps the body straight whilst cooking.

Put a large pan of salted water onto boil and have ready a large bowl of iced water. Boil the large claws for $2^1/_2$ minutes (timing from when the water returns to the boil) then remove from the pan with large tongs and plunge into the cold water. Add the skewered bodies and cook for just 30 seconds. Remove to the iced water.

Crack the claws with a lobster cracker. Snap back the black tipped top claw and then push it up to release the segment of lobster meat. Crack open the main claw, and pull out the meat.

To perpare the tail meat, turn the shell on its back and using sharp scissors, snip along the underbelly on both sides. Pull off the under shell, then turn the tail over and using a heavy cook's knife cut down between the segments of the shell into 'tronconnettes'.

## *Finish the dish*

Boil the stock until reduced by half then add the cream and set aside.

Cook the noodles and toss with some butter.

When ready to serve, heat the grill until hot. Brush the lobster meat tronconnettes with a drizzle of olive oil then season and sprinkle with some lemon juice. Grill until hot and sprinkle with a little more lemon juice.

Divide the noodles between four warmed plates and sit the lobster claws on top. Arrange the Troncettes around the side.

Reheat the sauce and froth with an electric hand held blender. Pour around the lobster and noodles and serve garnished with parsley leaves.

# Sea Bream with Crab Couscous and Red Pepper Sauce

Serves 4

*Aubergine Caviar (page 23)*
*2 red peppers, cored seeded and*
  *chopped*
*1 clove garlic, chopped*
*500 ml Chicken Stock (page 29)*
*A good knob of butter*
*4 x 160g sea bream fillets – skin on*
*A little plain flour, for dusting*
*Olive oil, for frying*

**For the Crab Couscous**
*250ml Vegetable Stock (page 33)*
*150g instant couscous*
*A good pinch saffron strands, crushed*
*125g white crabmeat*
*10 large fresh basil leaves, shredded*
*Juice 1 lemon*
*2 tablespoons lemon oil*

Make the couscous first. Boil 250ml of stock and mix with the couscous and saffron strands in a large bowl. Cover with Clingfilm and set aside to allow the stock to be absorbed, about 10 minutes.

Make the Aubergine Caviar.

Make the sauce by simmering together the chopped peppers and garlic in a third of the chicken stock until softened then add the remaining stock and continue cooking until reduced down again. Blitz in a blender or food processor and rub through a sieve with the back of a ladle. Return the smooth sauce to a pan, reheat gently and whisk in the butter. Set aside.

Fork through the crabmeat for any flecks of shell, then mix the crabmeat into the couscous with the basil and half the lemon juice. Add a couple of tablespoons of lemon oil and heat gently in a saucepan, stirring with a fork. Check the seasoning.

When ready to serve, season the fish on both sides and dust with flour. Heat some olive oil in a non-stick pan, add the fish, skin side down, and cook for 2–3 minutes until crisp then flip over carefully and leave in the pan for 2–3 minutes to cook in the residual heat. Sprinkle with more lemon juice and salt to taste.

Divide the warm couscous between four plates, place the fish on top, spoon around aubergine caviar and the sauce and serve immediately.

# Meat, Game and Poultry

# Calves Liver Lyonnaise with Sauté Potatoes

*Any dish that mentions Lyonnaise in the title will include lots of onions – slow-cooked until they become deliciously caramelised, the ideal accompaniment to calves liver.*

Serves 4

3 large onions, thinly sliced
3–4 tablespoons olive oil plus extra
    for sautéing
150 ml red wine
250ml Veal Stock (page 32)
4 large even-sized Maris Piper
    potatoes, about 1 kg

500g calves liver, sliced in four
    lengthways about 1cm thick
50g plain flour
Crisp-fried parsley sprigs (page 24)
Sea salt and freshly ground black
    pepper

Place the onions in a large pan and cook very gently in the oil until the natural juices start to run and the onions begin to brown and caramelise, up to about 40–45 minutes.

Pour the wine into a pan and boil until reduced by two thirds then add the veal stock and cook until reduced to about 150ml. Set aside.

Meanwhile, peel the potatoes – if you want perfect rounds cut in half across the middle and press down on each half with a deep round cutter, 4–5cm in diameter, into cylinders. Then cut these cylinders into slices approximately 5mm thick.

When ready to cook the potatoes, pour enough oil into a saucepan to liberally coat the base and leave until you can feel a moderate heat rising then add the potatoes in a single layer. It is best to cook the potatoes in two batches rather than crowd the pan. Cook for about 3 minutes until golden brown before turning to cook the other side the same way. Check the potatoes are tender with the tip of a sharp knife. Drain on paper towel. Keep warm, uncovered, in a low oven so that they remain crisp.

Season the flour on a large plate and press the liver slices on both sides in the seasoned flour to coat – shake off the excess. In another frying pan, heat a thin layer of oil and fry the slices for about 1–2 minutes on each side until browned and crisp on the outside and pink and juicy on the inside.

Serve the liver on the onions with the crisp potatoes and red wine jus. Garnish with fried parsley sprigs.

# Beef and Bones with Chips

*We like to cook our fillet steaks on the bone, but you will have to pre-order this from your butcher before he bones out his beef. When cooked 'bone-in' the flavour of the bone infuses the meat and helps prevent it from shrinking back too much. You could use a T-bone steak as an alternative to fillet on the bone. Serve this simple dish with chunky handcut chips, some shallots in red wine sauce and drizzles of olive oil.*

Serves 4

*4 fillet steaks, on the bone, about 250g each*
*2 Maris Piper potatoes, about 250g each*
*Vegetable oil, for deep-frying*
*A large knob of butter*
*Crispy Parsley Leaves (page 24)*
*Shallots in Red Wine and Port (see below)*
*Sea salt and freshly ground black pepper*

Trim the steaks of any excess fat or sinew. Set aside until ready to serve. Make the Shallots in Red Wine and Port (see below).

For the chips, peel and cut the potatoes into neat 1cm thick sticks. (In the restaurant we actually cut ours into banana shapes, a process known as 'turning'). Soak in a large bowl of cold water for 5 minutes, then drain. Transfer the chips to a pan just covering them with salted water and cook on a low heat for five minutes and drain. The potatoes will start to get a slightly sticky feel to them. This is what will help form the crispiness to the chip. Heat a chip pan a third full of vegetable oil to 100°C. Plunge the potato sticks into the oil and cook for about 3 minutes until softened but still uncoloured. Drain well and cool.

When ready to serve, heat a heavy based frying pan until hot. Brush the steaks with a little oil and season both sides well. Fry for about 2 minutes each side until nicely browned, sliding in the knob of butter and spooning the hot butter over the steaks as they cook. Remove the steaks to a platter and allow to rest. For medium to well done steaks, allow about 4–5 minutes each side. The steaks carry on cooking whilst they rest, so take care not to overcook.

Back to the chips. Reheat the chip pan oil to 190°C. Lower in the blanched chips and cook for a further 3–4 minutes until golden and crisp then drain well on paper towel. Serve the steaks with the chips, parsley and Shallots in Red Wine and Port.

## Shallots in Red Wine and Port

*4 large (banana) shallots, chopped*
*2 cloves garlic, crushed*
*300ml red wine*
*100ml port*

Cook the shallots and garlic gently in the wine and port until the liquid is reduced right down and the shallots are very soft, about 20 minutes. Season and cool then shape into oval 'quenelles' using two teaspoons.

# Beef Bavette with Red Wine and Shallot Sauce

*Bavette steak (Onglet in French bistros, or Skirt in traditional British butchers) is a lean flavoursome cut from below the rib cage. It is perfect served with creamy mashed potatoes, braised cabbage and shallots in Red Wine Sauce.*

Serves 4

*1 quantity Red Wine Sauce (page 36)*
*1 kg Maris Piper potatoes, peeled*
*150g butter*
*3 tablespoons milk*
*1 Savoy cabbage*
*3 tablespoons Chicken Stock (page 29)*
*or water*
*2 large or 4 smaller shallots, finely diced*
*4 bavettes of beef, about 180g each, about 2.5 cm thick*
*Sea salt and pepper*

Make the Red Wine Sauce and set aside.

Cut the potatoes into even-sized chunks and boil in salted water for about 12 minutes until tender, then drain and return to the pan on the heat to dry off. Add 50g (a third) of the butter, the milk and seasoning then mash together until smooth. (Alternatively, if you have a potato ricer, press the potato through for perfect lump free mash).

For the cabbage, remove the outer leaves, cut in quarters and cut out the core then using a large knife, cut into fine shreds. Place in a large saucepan with the chicken stock or water and another 50g of butter. Heat until sizzling then cover the pan and cook on a medium heat for about 5–7 minutes until just softened. When just softened, remove from the heat, season and set aside.

Put the last 50g of butter and the diced shallots into a pan on a medium heat and sauté until the shallots have softened but not browned, about 10 minutes. Stir in the wine sauce and heat until bubbling.

Season the bavettes both sides with salt and pepper and cook in a hot frying pan with a little oil for about 1 minute each side, or more if you like your meat cooked further, but take care not to overcook. Remove and rest for at least 5 minutes.

To serve, cut each steak with the grain into four. Serve on a bed of the cabbage sprinkled with sea salt and pepper and the potato and sauce alongside.

# Salad of Black Pudding and Poached Eggs

*This recipe is inspired by Paul Heathcote, a great champion of traditional British dishes with a neat modern twist. We use his recipe for homemade black pudding using pork fat, lamb sweetbreads, sultanas and dried pigs blood – ingredients that are not the easiest to find in your supermarket or butcher. So I suggest you use a good traditional black pudding from Bury in Lancashire or Irish Clonakilty. Serve with some sautéed potatoes.*

Serves 4

*200ml Veal Jus (page 33)*
*Some Crispy Parsley Leaves (page 24)*
*300g good quality black pudding*
*A little oil for frying*
*4 slices pancetta*
*4 very fresh free range organic eggs*

*1 teaspoon vinegar, for poaching*
*150g mixed salad leaves*
*A little vinaigrette*
*Sea salt and freshly ground black pepper*

Make some reduced Veal Jus and Crispy Parsley Leaves and set aside.

Heat some oil in a frying pan and cook the pancetta rashers until crisp. Drain on paper towel and keep warm.

Slice the black pudding into 12 slices and fry for about 1–2 minutes each side until cooked and crisp. Set aside.

Poach the eggs in lightly salted water with the vinegar for about 2–3 minutes until the whites are firm and yolks still soft. Drain on paper towel and trim the whites to a neat shape. Reheat the Veal Jus.

Toss the salad leaves in vinaigrette and divide between four plates. Sit a poached egg on top with pancetta and Crispy Parsley Leaves. Put 3 slices of hot black pudding on each plate and drizzle around the Veal Jus. Serve immediately.

# Braised Blade of Beef Parmentier

*Blade of beef is another favourite cut of mine. A lean and tasty cut from the shoulder of a forequarter of beef, it is best slow-cooked a day ahead. A Parmentier is a French potato-topped meat pie. In Simpsons Restaurant, we make up mini pies by pressing the shredded meat and mashed potato into a metal ring and topping with a crispy fried potato galette, but you could make a larger family sized pie. Serve with baby leeks, carrots and turnips.*

Serves 6–8

*1 blade or brisket of beef, about
    1kg weight*
*2 large carrots, peeled and halved*
*2 sticks celery, halved*
*1 bulb garlic, halved*
*1 onion, quartered*
*2 sprigs thyme*
*10 black peppercorns*
*300ml Veal Stock (page 32)*

*1kg Maris Piper potatoes*
*3 tablespoons milk*
*75g butter, melted*
*Sea salt and freshly ground black
    pepper*

**To serve**
*Baby turnips, carrots and leeks*
*A knob of butter*

In a large ovenproof pan that can be heated on the hob (e.g. cast iron) with a lid, place the beef, carrots, celery, garlic, onion, thyme and peppercorns. Cover with cold water and bring to the boil. Meanwhile, heat the oven to its lowest setting, around 100°C, Gas Low.

Put the lid on the pan and place in the oven for up to 4 hours or until the beef is very soft and flakes when pressed with a fork. Remove from the heat and cool. Remove the beef from the liquor and break into fine shreds removing any fatty pieces.

Strain the liquor into another saucepan and boil to reduce to around 600ml. Discard the braising vegetables, then stir the Veal Stock into the beef liquor and boil down again to around 500ml.

Place the shredded beef in an ovenproof dish and add some of the reduced liquor to moisten and bind it together. Season to taste. The remaining liquor can be frozen and used as stock elsewhere.

Reserve two long potatoes and make creamy mash with the remaining potato. Peel and cut into even-sized chunks, then boil in salted water for about 15 minutes until just tender. Drain, return to the pan with the milk and half the butter, mashing together until smooth and creamy. Season and set aside.

Peel and thinly slice the reserved potato. Heat a large flat frying pan and arrange the slices in 4 neat overlapping rounds, about 10–12cm, drizzling with melted butter. Fry until golden brown and crisp for about 5 minutes each side turning gently with a palette knife so they remain in a round galette. Drain on paper towel.

Prepare and lightly blanche the baby vegetables in boiling salted water then drain and toss with more melted butter. Divide the shredded meat into six portions on a non-stick tray pressed into 2–3cm deep, 10cm metal rings. Spoon over the mashed potato and level the tops.

When ready to serve, reheat the pies in the oven set at 180°C, Gas 4 for about 15 minutes until piping hot then using a palette knife, transfer to a dinner plate and lift off the metal rings. Fit a potato galette on top. Reheat the left over liquor and swirl around the plate to serve.

# Braised Shoulder of Lamb, Coco Beans, Courgettes, Dried Tomatoes, Lamb Jus

*From the end of June through to early autumn we buy in bags of semi-dried coco beans from France. Similar to fresh borlotti beans they are quite delicious and perfect served alongside tender braised lamb shanks.*

Serves 4

*150g semi-dried coco beans*
*2 carrot, halved*
*2 sticks celery, halved*
*1 onion, halved*
*4 lamb shoulder shanks (Klefticos)*
*About 3 tablespoons olive oil*
*1 leek, halved*
*2 sprigs thyme*

*1 sprig rosemary*
*10 cloves Garlic Confit (page 25)*
*A good knob of butter*
*2 large courgettes*
*6 plum tomatoes*
*Sea salt and freshly ground black*
  *pepper*

Precook the beans in enough cold water to cover along with the carrots, celery and onion until tender, about 25 minutes, then drain and remove the vegetables. Set aside.

Brush the lamb shanks with some oil and brown in a large cast iron casserole, turning them to brown evenly and adding a little extra oil if necessary. Add the remaining vegetables including the leeks plus 1 sprig of thyme and rosemary and two of the garlics.

Cover with cold water, add seasoning and bring to the boil. Make sure the water is at least 5cm above the vegetables etc. Heat the oven to 140°C, Gas 1, cover and transfer the pan to the oven and bake for about 2 hours until the meat is tender.

Remove the shanks with a slotted spoon and place on a roasting pan and return to the oven, uncovered for 15–20 minutes. Strain off the cooking liquor into a saucepan. Remove and discard the vegetables and herbs. Add a knob of butter to the beans, season, reheat and keep warm.

For the courgette rounds, cut 5mm thick strips from the outside of the courgettes. Then cut these into rounds about 3cm. Boil in salted water for 2–3 minutes. Drain and toss in some more butter.

Blanch the tomatoes in boiling water for 7 seconds and remove and refresh in cold water for 10 seconds. Peel the skin from the tomatoes, cut them in half and remove the seeds. Toss in a bowl with some olive oil and a sprig of thyme. Lay them on a tray and cook at around 100°C, Gas Low for 3 hours until they begin to wrinkle.

Boil the lamb liquor until reduced to around 200ml then strain again and check the seasoning. Serve the shanks with the beans and lamb jus surrounded by the courgettes, tomatoes and cloves of Garlic Confit.

# Fried Veal Chop, Glazed Navets & Creamed Madiera Sauce

*Summer is the time for navets (long baby turnips) – they make for a perfect accompaniment to a juicy veal chop. The Madeira Sauce has cream added making it appear intriguingly like a café au lait. The recipe also works very well with pork chops.*

Serves 4

*200ml Madeira Sauce (page 37)*
*24 baby navets, about 250g total weight*
*50g butter*
*4 veal chops, about 225g each*

*A little olive oil, for frying*
*3–4 tablespoons double cream*
*1 tablespoon chopped fresh chives*
*Sea salt and freshly ground black pepper*

First, make the Madeira Sauce and then set aside.

Next, lightly peel the navets and cook in salted boiling water, for about 5 minutes until just tender but still firm. Toss with the butter and keep warm.

Heat a large frying pan on a medium heat, season the chops, add a little drizzle of oil to the pan and fry for 5–6 minutes each side until just firm but not overcooked. Remove the chops from the pan and pour in the Madeira Sauce. Stir in the cream and bring to the boil, stirring briskly. Pour the sauce through a fine sieve and keep warm.

Serve the chops drizzled with the sauce and the navets sprinkled with the chives. Pasta would be perfect with this.

# Veal Medallions Wrapped in Parma Ham with Creamed Macaroni and Marjoram Sauce

*This recipe uses tender veal fillet wrapped in Parma ham which is then roasted. If veal is not available then use pork tenderloin. You will also need to get some long macaroni, known in Italy as zitonni.*

Serves 4

600–700g fillet of veal
200g thinly sliced Parma ham
200ml Madeira Sauce (page 37)
2 sprigs fresh marjoram plus extra
  leaf tips to garnish
1 large red pepper
12–16 stoned black olives
8 lengths of zitonni pasta (large

macaroni tubes)
A little olive oil
A knob of butter
1 tablespoon Parmesan cheese
2 tablespoons double cream
4 Semi-dried Tomatoes (page 26)
Sea salt and freshly ground black
  pepper

Season the veal with pepper only and roll as tight as you can in the Parma ham. Overwrap tightly in Clingfilm and chill.

Make the Madeira Sauce and add the marjoram sprigs to infuse.

Cut the pepper into 2cm wide strips and grill until the skin starts to burn. Remove from the heat and peel the skin off and place in a heatproof dish along with the olives. This makes them easy to reheat under the grill when ready to serve.

Cook the pasta until al dente, then drain and run under cold water. Drain again and cut into 20cm lengths. Set aside.

Put the veal loin (still in Clingfilm) into a pan of boiling water for 3 minutes and then remove. Cool slightly and unwrap. Heat a large frying pan until hot and add a little oil and a knob of butter. Roll the loin in the hot pan to seal and brown the Parma ham then lower the heat and cook for about 8 minutes until the centre is still slightly pink. Remove and rest for a few minutes.

Preheat a grill. Roll the pasta with the cheese and cream and place in a shallow dish under the grill to just brown the top.

Reheat the sauce then remove the marjoram. Slice the veal roll into medallions and serve with the pasta, the red pepper cubes, olives, tomato and sauce. Garnish with the marjoram leaf tips.

# Poached and Grilled Poulet Noir with Root Vegetables, Wild Rice and Sauce Suprème

*If you detach the legs and backbones from a chicken you are left with only the breasts still attached to the ribcage. This is known as a 'chicken crown' which we poach first in stock and then remove in one piece to brown under a hot grill. This method gives you the best of both worlds – moist, tender chicken breast with delicious crispy skin. I use the French Poulet Noir or Label Rouge birds, but there are some excellent British chickens now sold under the Label Anglais brand. The Sauce Suprème is a Chicken Veloute with some fresh foie gras whisked in. For the stock base you could use the poaching liquor the breasts were par-cooked in (if you don't have time to make a chicken stock).*

Serves 4

100g wild rice
About 75g butter
500ml Chicken Stock (page 29)
$^1/_2$ small onion, chopped roughly
1 carrot, chopped
1 stick celery, chopped
1 sprig thyme
1 clove garlic
2 'crowns' of chicken (see above)
250ml Chicken Veloute sauce (page 41)

100g foie gras, cut into small cubes
Sea salt and freshly ground black
  pepper

**Vegetable garnish**
4 small sticks of celery
4 baby turnips
4 baby leeks
2 carrots

Put the rice into a large pan and cover with at least a litre of boiling water. Return to the boil and cook for about 40 minutes until many of the grains have split. Drain, return to the pan and toss with a little of the butter. (Wild rice requires more water and longer cooking than normal rice).

Put the chicken stock in a pan with the chopped onion, carrot, celery, thyme and garlic. Bring to the boil then simmer gently for 5 minutes. Submerge one chicken crown under the stock, breasts side down and poach for 8–10 minutes until just firm. Repeat with the second crown.

Strain the stock and make the Chicken Veloute. Then, whisk in the foie gras until it melts. Set the sauce aside.

Prepare the vegetable garnish. The carrots should be peeled, split lengthways and the core cut out, then the flesh cut in 2–3cm lengths. Blanch all the vegetables in boiling salted water (or extra stock) for 2–3 minutes, drain and toss with a little extra butter.

When ready to serve, heat a grill until hot. Remove the breasts whole from the carcass, with a little of the wing bone attached. Brush the skin lightly with some oil and grill until the skin is golden and crisp. Reheat the rice, sauce and vegetables. Serve the chicken on the rice, with the sauce poured around and vegetables alongside.

# Roast Gressingham Duck, Bok Choi, Glazed Apple, Celeriac Purée, Honey & Cracked Pepper Sauce

*Roasting a whole duck is tricky if the legs and breasts are to be tender without overcooking. We separate the legs and 'confit' them slowly in duck fat and then slow fry the breasts in a pan. This dish is served with 3 garnishes which can all be made ahead.*

Serves 4

2 Gressingham ducks, about 2kg each
400g duck or goose fat
Honey and Cracked Pepper Sauce
  (page 38)
1 celeriac, about 500g
About 300ml milk
1 large Cox apple
50g butter

1 tablespoon sugar
1 tablespoon lemon juice
2 bok choi
A few potato crisps, to serve,
  preferably homemade or hand-fried
Sea salt and freshly ground black
  pepper

Cut off the duck legs (with thighs attached) then slice off the four whole breasts. Chill the breasts but place the legs in a deep sided pan and pour over the duck or goose fat. Heat to a temperature of around 90–100°C, this will be on a low heat if you don't have a thermometer. Season and cook for about $2^{1}/_{2}$ hours until the meat is very tender. Then remove and cool. These can be cooked ahead and reheated to serve.

Meanwhile make the Honey and Cracked Pepper Sauce and set aside.

Make the celeriac purée. Peel and chop the celeriac then place in a saucepan with the milk and 300ml water. Season and bring to the boil, then simmer until tender, about 15 minutes. Drain and blitz the celeriac in a blender or food processor until smooth and creamy.

For the glazed apple, first peel thinly then cut the four sides off the apple around the core. Place the sides down on a board and using a 5cm cutter cut each into rounds. Place in a microwave proof bowl with the butter, sugar, lemon juice and 2 tablespoons of water. Cover with Clingfilm, allowing a small vent and cook on medium power for 2–3 minutes. Remove and stand a few minutes and then set aside.

Trim the base of the bok choi, simmer in a little salted boiling water for 1–2 minutes and keep warm with the apple.

Cook the duck breasts – place them skin side down in a cold frying pan and start to heat it slowly over a medium heat. As the fat starts to run, pour it off – it can be saved for another use. When the skin becomes nice and crisp and the flesh is three quarters cooked (about 7 minutes) turn the meat over onto the flesh side and cook for about 2 minutes more until the flesh feels lightly springy when pressed. Remove the breasts from the pan and season. Leave to rest in a low oven.

## To *finish and serve*

Reheat the duck legs under a low grill until the skin crisps. Reheat the celeriac and sauce. Slice the duck breasts into medallions. Scoop the celeriac into quenelles, place on warm dinner plates and garnish with crisps. Arrange the duck legs on bok choi with the breast medallions around. Garnish with a glazed apple round each. Spoon around the sauce and serve.

# Rack of Lamb with Pistachio Crust, Fondant Potatoes, Artichoke Purée and Basil Sauce

*You need a rack of lamb trimmed in the French style, i.e. the top bones scraped clean. The pistachio crust is made with ground green pistachios that are pressed onto the back of the lamb and grilled until crisp. Fondant potatoes are first cut into an even barrel shape then roasted in the oven with butter and stock. Serve with lightly boiled green beans.*

Serves 4

*2 x 6 bone racks of lamb*
*200ml Lamb Jus (page 34)*
*80g unsalted (green) shelled*
  *pistachio nuts*
*250g butter*
*2 large globe artichokes*
*A little lemon juice*
*3–4 clove garlics, crushed*
*About 600ml Chicken or Vegetable*
  *Stock (pages 29 and 33)*
*2–3 tablespoons double cream*

*2 large potatoes, ideally Maris Piper*
*A little olive oil*
*6–7 sprigs fresh thyme, plus extra to*
  *garnish*
*20g basil leaves, finely shredded*
*250g whole green beans, topped*
  *and tailed*
*4 Garlic Confit (page 25)*
*Sea salt and freshly ground black*
  *pepper*

Ensure the lamb racks are neatly trimmed and the top bones scraped clean. Make the Lamb Jus and set aside.

For the pistachio crust, grind the nuts in a blender or food processor until coarsely chopped. Heat 75g of the butter in a small pan until it starts to foam and then mix in the nuts. Remove and cool to a paste.

Make the artichoke purée. Trim off all the leaves, remove the spiky choke and roughly chop the firm heart. Drop in some cold water with a little lemon juice then drain.

Sauté the hearts in a knob of butter with 1 clove garlic for about 2–3 minutes then add about 4 tablespoons of stock. Cover, season and simmer for 12 minutes until tender, then uncover and add 2–3 tablespoons of cream and season. Blitz in a food processor until smooth and rub through a fine sieve with the back of a spoon or ladle.

For the potatoes, heat the oven to 180°C, Gas 4. Peel the potatoes thinly and trim to an even barrel shape, pressing down with a metal round cutter about 4cm diameter then cut into two equal cylinders. Brown both ends in a small frying pan in a little hot oil and remove to a small roasting or baking dish that is about 5cm tall, or the height of the potatoes. Press the best end of the potatoes onto the base so that they cook to a golden brown. Melt 150g of the remaining butter and pour over the potato then add the remaining garlic, thyme sprig and seasoning. Pour in the remaining stock which should come at least three-quarters of the way up and bake for about 30 minutes, basting the potatoes 3–4 times until the stock has been absorbed and the potatoes are tender. Keep warm.

Leave the oven on. Seal the racks in a little oil in a hot frying pan on top of the stove then transfer to an ovenproof dish, top with the remaining thyme sprigs and roast for 8–10 minutes. Season, remove and cool for 10 minutes. When cool, press the pistachio paste onto the top of the racks.

When ready to serve, heat the grill to low and cook the crusted racks for about 5 minutes until hot and crisp.

Reheat the Lamb Jus and stir in the shredded basil. Lightly boil the green beans and toss with the last of the butter.

Spoon artichoke purée in the centre of four warmed dinner plates and top with green beans. Cut each lamb rack in half and place on the beans. Serve with the fondant potato garnished with a confit garlic and thyme sprig, if liked. Drizzle the sauce around and serve immediately.

# Lamb Shanks with Chick Peas, Swiss Chard and Gremolata

*This is another simple classic rustic dish that would be perfect for a Sunday lunch. The shanks are best cooked the day before and left to cool in the liquor. Swiss chard could be substituted with large leaf (but not baby size) spinach or even spring greens.*

Serves 4

*1 leek*
*1 onion, peeled*
*2 carrots*
*4 large lamb shanks*
*10 peppercorns*
*3 cloves garlic, lightly crushed*
*1 bay leaf*
*1 sprig fresh thyme*
*A little olive oil*

*A little clear honey*
*1 bunch Swiss chard*
*A squeeze of lemon juice*
*A good knob of butter*
*200g cooked (or canned and drained) chick peas*
*2 tablespoons Gremolata (page 22)*
*Sea salt and freshly ground black pepper*

Roughly chop the leek, onion and carrots. Place in a large flameproof casserole with the shanks, peppercorns, garlic, bay and thyme. Cover with cold water, add some salt to taste, bring to the boil then cover and cook on a gentle heat for $1^{1}/_{2}$–2 hours until the meat is very tender. Remove, cool and chill.

Next day, remove the shanks and set aside. Strain the liquor and boil down until reduced to 200ml. Set aside.

Heat the oven to 180°C, Gas 4. Brush the cooked lamb shanks with a little oil and roast for about 12 minutes until piping hot and lightly browned. Remove, brush with some honey and return to the oven for another 5 minutes. Remove and keep warm.

For the chard, cut the stalks from the leaves and slice into 2cm lengths. Roughly slice the leaves. Boil the stalks first in salted water with the lemon juice for 4 minutes. Drain and cook the chard leaves in fresh boiling, salted water for 1–2 minutes. Drain and shake dry. Heat a knob of butter in a frying pan and sauté the blanched chard for a minute or two and check the seasoning.

Heat the chick peas with the Gremolata and then add the lamb liquor. Serve the shanks, chard, chick peas and lamb juices together.

# Roast Rack of Pork, Glazed Apples and Cider Sauce

*A rack of pork is a French style half boned best end of pork loin with the rib bones scraped clean. You will have to ask your butcher to prepare one for you. This makes a brilliant Sunday roast joint.*

Serves 6

*1 rack of pork, boned and skin well
    scored, about 6 chops
Cider Sauce (page 38)
4 Granny Smith apples*

*50g butter
2 tablespoon clear honey
Sea salt and freshly ground black
    pepper*

Pre-heat oven to 220°C, Gas 6. Brush the scored pork rind with oil and season all over. Roast for 10 minutes then reduce the heat to 170°C, Gas 3. Continue roasting until thoroughly cooked, about 1–1$\frac{1}{2}$ hours depending upon the size of pork.

Meanwhile, make the sauce and set aside.

Peel and core the apples then cut into even slices. Heat the butter in a large frying pan and add the apples. Cook until lightly golden and softened then mix in the honey and turn to coat them in the juices.

Serve with roast or Fondant Potatoes (page 134) and buttered cabbage.

# Roast Squab Pigeon 'Pierre Orsi'

*This is a recipe from the Lyons chef, Pierre Orsi, who trained under the legendary Paul Bocuse. A squab pigeon is especially reared for the plate, unlike the darker meat wood pigeons, so is rather more delicate in flavour. If you can't find any squab then use one hen pheasant instead of two pigeons.*

Serves 4

200ml Pigeon Sauce (page 43)
4 squab pigeons, about 600g each
12 cloves rose garlic
300ml duck fat
120g wild rice
400ml Chicken Stock (page 29)
1 small Savoy cabbage

1 teaspoon bicarbonate of soda, optional
8 large oyster mushrooms, sliced
4 cloves Garlic Confit (page 25)
A knob of butter
Sea salt and freshly ground black pepper

Make the pigeon sauce and set aside. Cut off the legs from the pigeon so you have a 'crown' of breasts still attached to the rib cage and put into a pan with the garlic and the duck fat.

Cook the legs – melt the duck fat over a gentle heat and then bring it to the boil. Cover and place at the edge of a very low hob ring so it remains at about 90°C for 45 minutes. Allow the legs to cool in the fat then remove and wipe off excess fat.

Cook the wild rice, by placing in a small saucepan with the stock. Bring to the boil, then cover and simmer gently for about 40–45 minutes until tender and many of the grains have burst open. Drain and set aside.

Quarter the cabbage and remove the cores. Take the medium green leaves from the cabbage and remove all of the veins from them and shred all the leaves. Put the shredded cabbage into a pan of boiling water to blanch it for 30 seconds. Add the teaspoon of bicarbonate of soda to help to keep the cabbage green. Drain and return to the pan with a spoonful or two of the duck fat from the pigeon legs. Season and keep warm.

When ready to cook the pigeon breasts, heat the oven to 190°C, Gas 5. Heat a little more of the duck fat in a frying pan and seal the crowns of the bird with the breasts still attached, pressing the skin down to golden brown. Place in a small roasting pan, season and roast for about 5 minutes. Reheat the legs at the same time.

Remove the breasts from the oven, rub with a knob of butter and rest for 5 minutes. Use a small, very sharp knife to cut off each breast.

Using the roasting pan with the juices, quickly sauté the mushrooms until just softened and then season.

To serve, reheat the Pigeon Sauce until boiling. Serve two legs and two breasts per portion with the cabbage, wild rice, mushrooms, garlic confits and sauce spooned around.

# Roast Loin of Rabbit, Confit Leg, Chestnut and Potato Mash, Cabbage and Juniper Sauce

*Good butchers still sell whole farmed French rabbits, ready for roasting. Ask for the legs to be removed and the saddles detached.*

Serves 4

1 rabbit, about 1.5 kg each – cut into 2 legs and 2 saddles
400g can duck or goose fat
2 sprigs thyme
4 cloves garlic
2 bay leaves
1 quantity of Juniper Sauce (page 50)
2 large potatoes, about 300g each
50g butter

3–4 tablespoons unsweetened chestnut purée
1 Savoy cabbage
1 carrot
$^1/_2$ small celeriac
2–4 tablespoons Mascarpone
Sea salt and freshly ground black pepper

Cut out the loin fillets from the rabbit saddles, trim and set aside. Put the hind legs in a pan with the goose or duck fat, thyme, garlic and bay leaves. Heat until the fat begins to bubble slightly or until it reaches 100°C and leave at this temperature for about 3 hours until very tender. (The forequarter legs can be confitted slowly in some more duck or goose fat, then shredded and covered in a little fat for Rilletes).

Make the sauce using the rabbit carcasses, if possible, and set aside.

Peel the potato, cut in chunks and boil in salted water until just tender, about 15 minutes. Drain, return to the pan and mash with half the butter until smooth and creamy. Mix in the chestnut purée, add seasoning and keep warm.

For the cabbage, quarter and cut out the cores then shred the leaves finely. Peel the carrot and celeriac and cut into julienne sticks.

Blanch the cabbage, carrot and celeriac separately in a pan of boiling water for 1–2 minutes each, then drain and return to the pan with the Mascarpone and seasoning.

When ready to serve, heat a little duck fat in a frying pan and brown the rabbit loins evenly. Continue cooking in the pan or place in a hot oven set at 220°C, Gas 7 for about 4 minutes. Remove and rest for 5 minutes before slicing.

Serve each portion with a leg and sliced loin on a bed of Mascarpone vegetables accompanied by the chestnut potato. Reheat the jus and pour around.

# Roast Pheasant with Pineapple Sauerkraut, Foie Gras and Spatzle

*This German inspired dish is perfect for the autumn when the pheasant season starts. You will need to make some easy fresh spatzle (pasta). Sauerkraut, sold in jars, goes surprisingly well with pineapple.*

**Serves 4**

*2 eggs*
*100g plain flour*
*A little milk, if necessary*
*200g canned sauerkraut*
*Some olive oil*
*1 brace pheasant, a hen and cock,*

*about 1kg each bird*
*100g diced fresh pineapple*
*100g fresh foie gras, diced*
*50g butter*
*Sea salt and freshly ground black*
*   pepper*

First, make the spatzle. Put the 2 eggs and the flour into a bowl and whisk for 7–8 minutes until the batter forms little air bubbles at the surface and pops. The more you whisk, the tighter the batter will get. If you find it gets too tight, add a splash of milk to let it down a little.

Have ready a large pan of salted boiling water. If you have a spatzle maker, rub the batter through the holes with a spatula so it drops into the water below. It will cook in seconds as little squiggles of pasta. If you don't have a special mould, then rub the batter through a colander using the back of a ladle over the pan. Remove the spatzle as it rises to the surface with a slotted spoon into a large bowl of iced water, then drain again and toss with a little oil.

Drain the sauerkraut and rinse it under a cold tap and shake well to drain. Place in a saucepan with the pineapple and season.

For the pheasants, heat the oven to 200°C, Gas 6. Put a drizzle of oil in a large frying pan and when it gets hot press in the pheasants on the breast skin sides first to colour. Then roll and move the pheasants around the pan to colour all the skin. You will need to protect your hands with a thick cloth. When browned, transfer the bird to a small roasting pan and roast for 7–8 minutes. Remove from the oven, season and allow to rest for least 5 minutes.

Heat the sauerkraut and pineapple until piping hot and set aside to keep warm.

Get another frying pan hot and add the diced foie gras. As it starts to brown, toss in the spatzle and butter and mix together well. Season and divide between 4 warmed plates. Carve the breasts from the pheasants, and cut off the legs using poultry shears. Serve with the sauerkraut.

# Croustillant of Pigeon, Confit of Cabbage and Garlic, Pigeon Jus

*A croustillant looks like a large cracker of filo – this recipe uses pigeon breasts and spinach as the filling. Use the legs and bones to make the accompanying jus.*

**Serves 4**

*4 x pigeon breasts*
*1 quantity of Pigeon Sauce (page 43)*
*60g foie gras*
*4 large leaves of spinach*
*8 sheets filo pastry*
*100g melted butter*
*¹/₂ Savoy cabbage*

*16 baby carrots*
*1 shallot, finely chopped*
*1–2 tablespoons duck or goose fat*
*8 Garlic Confit (page 25)*
*A little duck or goose fat*
*Sea salt and freshly ground black*
  *pepper*

Cut the 4 breasts from the pigeons, in whole fillets. Peel off the skin and season well.

Chop the remaining carcass which can be used to make the Pigeon Sauce (page 43). Slice the foie gras in two and put between the breasts in opposite directions, thick ends to thin so that you have 2 breast 'sandwiches'.

Now wrap the breasts in spinach leaves covering completely. Brush the sheets of filo pastry with melted butter and wrap the pigeon in 2 sheets of filo pastry like a half cracker and brush the tops with more butter.

To cook the cabbage, cut in two quarters, remove the cores and slice thinly. Blanch in boiling salted water for 2 minutes then drain and shake dry. Peel the carrots and boil until tender, then drain.

Gently sweat the chopped shallot until softened in the fat. Toss in the blanched cabbage, season and cook for another 3–4 minutes.

Meanwhile, heat the oven to 180°C, Gas 4, then bake the pigeon parcels on a baking sheet for about 12–15 minutes until crisp and golden. Remove and allow to rest for a good 5 minutes. Divide the cabbage between four warmed plates. Sit a croustillant on top, reheat the carrots and place alongside with the garlic confits. Reheat the sauce and pour on the plate. Serve immediately.

# Roast Guinea Fowl with its own Pastilla, Hazelnuts, Green Beans, Celeriac Purée and Guinea Fowl Jus

*A Pastilla is a light pigeon pie from North Africa. It uses the wafer-thin feuille de brik pastry which you can buy in Tunisian and Moroccan delis. Or you can use filo pastry. This is my version using the milder guinea fowl.*

Serves 4

*2 guinea fowl, about 1kg each*
*400g duck or goose fat*
*2 sprigs of thyme*
*1 bay leaf*
*1 cinnamon stick*
*2 cloves garlic, lightly crushed*
*2 teaspoons clear honey*
*1 tablespoon chopped fresh parsley*
*2 sheets of filo pastry or feuille de brik*
*A little melted butter or olive oil*

*Game Bird Jus (page 30)*
*1 small celeriac*
*300ml milk*
*A little double cream*
*200g whole green beans, topped and tailed*
*40g skinned hazelnuts, roughly chopped*
*A knob of butter*
*Sea salt and freshly ground black pepper*

Cut the guinea fowl legs from the body and place in a saucepan. Add the duck or goose fat, thyme, bay leaf, cinnamon and garlic. Heat until the oily fat starts to move slightly and registers a temperature of around 90°C. Turn the heat to low, partially cover the pan and leave for about 3 hours ensuring the oil doesn't get too hot or start to bubble. The legs should cook very slowly.

When the meat is very tender, remove from the pan with a slotted spoon and cool. Then pick off the meat and shred finely. Mix the meat in a bowl with the honey, parsley and seasoning. (If the bird came with any liver, you could lightly fry these then chop and mix in too).

To make the pastilles, cut the pastry sheets in long strips about 10–12cm wide, so you have 4 long strips. Spoon a quarter of the meat mixture at the end of one strip in a triangular mound, then lifting up the pastry underneath flip over to form another triangular shape partially enclosing the filling. Continue flipping the mound over so you eventually have a samosa or turnover shape. Brush the end of the pastry with some water and press to seal. Place join side down on a non-stick baking sheet.

Make 3 more samosa shape pies with the remaining filling and pastry sheets. Brush with some melted butter or oil then chill until ready to cook and serve.

Make the Game Bird Jus and set aside.

Peel the celeriac and cut into small chunks. Boil gently in the milk with 300ml water and seasoning until soft, then drain (retaining a little of the cooking liquor). Blitz to a smooth purée in a blender or food processor adding a little of the liquor if necessary.

Season to taste and add a little double cream if liked. Return to the pan for re-heating.

When ready to serve, cook the pastillas and guinea fowl breasts. Heat the oven to 200°C, Gas 6. Bake the pastilles for about 10–15 minutes until golden and crisp. Remove and cool.

Roast the guinea fowl breasts. Heat a frying pan with a little olive oil and when hot, press in the fowl on each side to brown the breast skin. Remove to a small roasting pan and season. Place in the oven for 6–8 minutes to cook, then remove and rest for 5 minutes. Carve off the whole breasts.

Reheat the Game Bird Jus. Blanch the green beans in boiling salted water until lightly cooked and still a little crisp. Drain and shake dry. Heat the hazelnuts in a small frying pan with a knob of butter and toss in the beans. Season and stir fry lightly.

Serve the pastillas with the celeriac purée, breasts and green beans. Drizzle the jus around and serve.

# Desserts

# A Few Sweet Basics

## *Puff Pastry*

*Although bought puff pastry is freely available we prefer to make our own because the flavour is more buttery and the texture more tender. Make a big batch and cut into 3 portions. Wrap and freeze unused portions.*

Makes about 1.2 kg

*400g butter, chilled*         *sifted with a good pinch of salt*
*500g strong white (bread) flour*    *250ml ice-cold water*

Rub 100g of butter into the flour, then mix in the water to make a dough. Cover with Clingfilm and chill for 20 minutes.

Pat out the remaining butter into a rectangle about 1cm thick (this can done done between sheets of Clingfilm). Roll out the rested dough to a third longer than the butter. Place the butter on the lower three quarters.

Fold over the top dough then fold the bottom third up to form a sandwich of 3 layers of dough and 2 layers of butter. Roll out to the size of the original rectangle. Then repeat the folding and rolling once more. Make sure the butter doesn't seep out. Cover and chill for another 20 minutes.

Roll, fold and turn a further 4 times, resting in between. You can cut the dough into 3 and freeze whatever you don't use for another time.

# Nut Tuiles

*75g butter, softened*
*75g caster sugar*
*1 egg, lightly beaten*

*2 teaspoons plain flour*
*75g finely ground hazelnuts or*
    *almonds*

Cream together the butter and sugar then gradually beat in the egg.

Mix in the flour and nuts to a soft paste then chill the mixture until firm.

Heat the oven to 180° C, Gas 4. Cover a large baking sheet with non-stick baking parchment and spread teaspoonfuls of the mixture thinly into 8cm rounds, spacing well apart. (In the restaurant we use a plastic stencil, which can be simply made from the lid of an old ice cream tub).

Bake for 6–8 minutes until golden.

Remove from the oven, stand for a few seconds before sliding off with a palette knife onto a wire rack to cool. Repeat with remaining mixture. For curled tuiles, press whilst still warm over a rolling pin. Cool on a wire tray then store in an airtight tin.

# Dried Fruit Slices
# (e.g. Bananas and Strawberries)

*Fruits used for these slices should be firm and slightly under ripe so that you can cut them as thinly as possible.*

*50g caster sugar*

*2 teaspoons lemon juice*

*1 slightly under ripe banana or 6–8*
*firm red strawberries*

Make a sugar syrup by dissolving the sugar in 3 tablespoons of boiling water. Add the lemon juice and cool. Heat the oven to its lowest setting.

Slice the fruits as wafer thin as possible using a serrated knife.

Lay a silicone non-stick mat on a baking tray. Dip the fruit slices in the syrup, drain and lay on the tray then bake for about $1^{1}/_{2}$ hours, turning once until crisp. Remove and cool. Store in an airtight container.

# Chocolate Sauce

*100g caster sugar*

*60g cocoa powder*

*Mix the sugar and cocoa in a saucepan and pour in 120ml water. Heat gently, stirring often until dissolved and smooth. Bubble for a few seconds until thickened, then cool, stirring occasionally to stop a skin forming.*

# Caramel Sauce

*100g caster sugar*
*50g liquid glucose*
*250ml double cream*

*2 tablespoons Calvados, optional*
*$^1/_2$ stick cinnamon, crushed*

Dissolve the sugar and glucose in 3 tablespoons of water over a low heat. When clear, bring to a boil and cook to a golden caramel colour.

Immediately remove from the heat and stir in a quarter of the cream, using a long handled wooden spoon. Then mix in another quarter along with the cinnamon and Calvados, if using.

Add the remaining cream then return to the boil, remove from the heat and leave to infuse for 20 minutes. Strain through a sieve, cool and use.

# Apricot Glaze

*It is well worth making up a jar of this to have to hand. It keeps very well*

*1 jar good quality apricot jam*

*A squeeze fresh lemon juice*

Scoop the jam into a pan. Add 2–3 tablespoons of water and a little lemon juice. Dissolve slowly until hot and runny then rub through a fine sieve with the back of a wooden spoon. Pour back into the jar and seal.

To use, simply warm until runny and brush on with a pastry brush.

# Coffee Macaroons with Mascarpone Cream

*All the stages of this dessert can be made ahead and put together just before serving. We also like to serve the macaroons with a scoop of Tiramisu Ice Cream and a drizzle of Espresso Syrup (page 178).*

Makes 8, to serve 4–8

*130g ground almonds*
*180g icing sugar, sifted (50g plus*
  *80g plus 50g)*
*3 large egg whites*
*1 tablespoon plus 1 tsp coffee*
  *essence, e.g. Camp Coffee*
*200ml Mascarpone*

*1 vanilla pod*

**To serve**
*A little sifted cocoa powder*
*8 Nut Tuiles (page 145) optional*
*A little cocoa powder, to dust*

Heat the oven to 130°C, Gas $\frac{1}{2}$. Cover a large baking tray with a non-stick mat or sheet of non-stick baking parchment.

Sift together the almonds and 50g of icing sugar. In an electric mixer with a whisk attachment, beat the egg whites until forming soft peaks then beat in 80g of icing sugar, a tablespoon at a time until stiff and glossy.

Using a large metal spoon, gently fold in the almond and sugar mix with the tablespoon of coffee essence to a shiny, smooth mixture.

Spoon the mixture into a piping bag fitted with a large plain nozzle and pipe out at least 16 x 6cm rounds, allowing room for expansion. Bake for around 25 minutes until a skin forms on top and the edges have a slight bubbly edge. Remove and cool. Lift off the baking paper and store in an air tight container.

When ready to serve, make the coffee cream – whisk together the Mascarpone, the remaining 50g of icing sugar and essence. Split open the vanilla pod and scrape out the seeds with the tip of a sharp knife and mix these in. If you have more than 16 macaroons, crush the remainders into small chunks and mix into the coffee cream.

Sandwich 8 macaroon 'sandwiches' with the coffee cream. Serve with a neat scoop of ice cream sitting on a tuile and the syrup swirled around. Dust with cocoa powder.

# Crème Caramel with Red Wine Pears

*This brings together two popular sweet dishes into one great dessert – a sure-fire favourite! We like to serve it with a scoop of Chocolate Ice Cream (page 179) or Sorbet (page 180) topped with a thin chocolate 'cigarette' but you could use bought chocolate sticks.*

Serves 8

**Red Wine Pears**
*1 x 75cl bottle red wine*
*525g caster sugar*
*1 cinnamon stick*
*1 vanilla pod*
*2 star anise*
*1 tablespoon pink peppercorns*
*8 small–medium pears, e.g.*
  *Williams, Roche or Comice*

*2 tablespoons liquid glucose*
*500ml milk*
*4 large egg yolks*
*125g sugar (100g plus 25g)*

**To serve, optional**
*Chocolate Ice Cream or Sorbet*
  *(pages 179 or 180)*
*8 small tuiles or some grated chocolate*
*8 chocolate sticks*

First, for the pears, make a syrup in a deep saucepan with the wine, 250ml of water and 400g sugar. Boil until the sugar dissolves then infuse with the spices.

Peel and core the pears and place in the boiling syrup. Return to a gentle boil then simmer, covered with a lid, for about 15 minutes, turning once or twice to ensure the pears are well submerged in the syrup and cook until al dente. Leave in the liquor to cool overnight then remove the pears with a slotted spoon. Cut each in quarters and cut out the cores. Make a sauce with the liquor by boiling it right down by at least three quarters until it coats the back of a spoon like a syrup. Strain and set aside.

For the crème caramels, sit 8 x 100ml dariole moulds in a deep roasting pan. Heat the oven to 140°C, Gas 1. Spoon the glucose into a heavy based saucepan with 100g sugar and 3 tablespoons water. Dissolve and then boil to a golden caramel. When the caramel is ready, pour into the bottom of the moulds.

Beat the yolks in a large heatproof bowl with the remaining 25g sugar. Bring the milk just to boiling point then pour onto the yolks, beating well. Strain through a conical sieve into the moulds.

Pour a kettle of boiling water into the roasting pan so the hot water comes two thirds the way up the sides of the darioles, then cook for 35 minutes or until just set but still a little wobbly. Remove the pan from the oven and allow to rest then remove the moulds from the bain marie, cool and chill.

To serve, demould the crème caramels and serve with pears, reduced syrup and scoops of Chocolate Ice Cream or Sorbet placed on small tuiles with a chocolate stick on top.

## When measuring liquid glucose

First warm the pot gently in the microwave for a few seconds.

# Fine Apple Tarts with Caramel Sauce

*Everyone loves apple tart! Try my lighter version – it is very easy. Serve warm with a scoop of homemade Sultana Ice Cream (page 180) in the centre.*

Serves 4

*200g puff pastry (page 144)*
*4 large Braeburn's or Cox's apples,*
  *peeled, cored and thinly sliced*
*50g butter, melted*

*3–4 tbsp caster sugar*
*Caramel Sauce or Apricot Glaze,*
  *(both page 147)*

Roll out the pastry to a 3mm thickness (depth of a £1 coin) then cut out 4 rounds about the size of a small saucer, about 12cm. Prick with a fork several times and leave to rest for 15 minutes on a non-stick baking tray whilst you heat the oven to 180°C, Gas 4.

Peel, core and thinly slice the apples and lay on the pastry rounds neatly overlapping leaving a 1cm edge. Brush with the melted butter and sprinkle with the sugar. Bake for about for 15 minutes until the edges are golden brown. Remove to a wire tray and cool. Brush with the Caramel Sauce or Apricot Glaze as they cool. Serve warm with scoops of Sultana Ice Cream and swirls of more Caramel Sauce.

# Gratin of Strawberries with Pink Champagne Sabayon

*This must be the ultimate strawberries and cream dessert. Except instead of whipped cream we spoon over a whisked pink Champagne sabayon froth that is then lightly grilled until caramelised. For a special treat, serve warm with scoops of our Luxury Vanilla Ice Cream (page 178).*

### Serves 4

*About 500g fresh strawberries*
*4 tablespoons pink Champagne*
*4 egg yolks*
*25g caster sugar*

*Squeeze fresh lemon juice*
*Dried strawberries (page 146), to*
*serve, optional*
*Luxury Vanilla Ice Cream (page 178)*

Wash the strawberries, if necessary and gently pat dry. Only do this at the last moment so they don't go soggy. Depending on the size of strawberries, halve or quarter if needed. Lay them out on four plates and preheat the grill.

Make the sauce. Put the Champagne, egg yolks, sugar and lemon juice into a heat proof bowl placed over a pan of gently simmering water. Using a large balloon whisk or hand held electric beater, whisk until you have a pale golden foam that has doubled in volume.

Spoon this over the strawberries to coat them evenly then place under the grill in batches until the sauce turns light golden and slightly crisp. Remove and serve with a scoop of ice cream in the centre, decorated with slices of dried strawberry if liked.

# Hot Spiced Cherries

*When fresh cherries are in season, poach them in a spicy red wine syrup and serve with small cubes of crunchy Pain d'Epice and pistachios. Serve with scoops of Pain d'Epice Ice Cream (page 180).*

**Serves 4**

| | |
|---|---|
| *300g fresh cherries* | *1 teaspoon pink peppercorns,* |
| *300ml red wine* | *optional* |
| *125g caster sugar* | *About ¹/₄ loaf Pain d'Epice (page 21)* |
| *1 vanilla pod* | *100g shelled green unsalted* |
| *1 cinnamon stick* | *pistachios* |
| *2 star anise* | *Pain d'Epice Ice Cream (page 180)* |

Stone the cherries using a stoning tool and place in a heatproof bowl.

Make the syrup. Heat the wine in a saucepan and add the sugar, stirring until dissolved. Add the vanilla pod, cinnamon, star anise and peppercorns, if using.

Simmer for 5 minutes then strain over the cherries and leave to cool and chill until required.

Cut one very thin slice of Pain d'Epice, remove crusts, cut into triangles and set aside. Then cut another thicker 1 cm slice and cut this into small cubes. Heat the oven to 160°C, Gas 3. Heat the cubes and triangles for 8 minutes. Remove the cubes to a rack and press the triangles over a rolling pin to cool.

Finely chop half the pistachios and set aside. Leave the rest whole.

To serve, reheat the cherries in juice until warm, not hot. Spoon the cherries onto a plate and drizzle over any extra juice. Scatter over the whole pistachios and bread cubes.

Spoon the chopped pistachios into small mounds on each plate and place a scoop of Pain d'Epice Ice Cream on top. Serve with a crisp spiced bread triangle on top.

# Chocolate Fondants

*Rich chocolate puddings are a dinner party favourite. These can be made ahead and you may need to buy a set of those fancy chefs' metal rings, although ramekins can be used and the fondants not turned out. In the restaurant we like to serve scoops of Avocado Ice Cream (page 181) alongside, and a chocolate fondant curl on top. You could use crisp Nut Tuiles (page 145) instead.*

**Makes 8**

*90g dark chocolate, preferably Valrhona, broken in pieces – see below*
*90g butter*
*2 free range eggs*

*2 egg yolks*
*40g caster sugar*
*40g plain flour, sifted*
*A little icing sugar sifted with some cocoa powder*

Melt the chocolate first: place in a large heatproof bowl with the butter over a pan of hot – not boiling – water and stir until dissolved. Remove from the heat and cool until lukewarm.

Whisk together the eggs, yolks, and sugar to a thick pale sabayon foam then fold this into the chocolate and finally sift in the flour and fold gently to combine.

Place 8 metal rings 6cm diameter and 4–5cm deep on a baking sheet and line each with buttered non-stick baking parchment. Pour in the mixture and chill until required.

Preheat the oven to 190°C, Gas 5. Bake the moulds for 20–22 minutes until risen and just firm to touch.

Remove from the rings and immediately slide the fondants onto dessert plates. Dust with icing sugar and cocoa powder. Serve with scoops of Avocado Ice Cream on tuiles.

## Cocoa solids

The flavour of this dessert depends on the quality of the chocolate you choose. Make sure to use one that has at least 60% cocoa solids marked on the pack. Personally I like to use Valrhona Guanaja, which has 70% cocoa solids.

# Almond and Apricot Tartlets with Amaretto Mascarpone

*These tartlets are made in three parts – pastry, fruit compote and a frangipane then all baked together. It can be made at least a day ahead to save time. We serve it with scoops of Mascarpone flavoured with almond flavoured Amaretto liqueur.*

**Serves 8**

250g *plain flour*
100g *icing sugar*
160g *ground almonds (25g plus 135g)*
260g *butter, at room temperature (125g plus 135g)*
3 *large free range eggs*
235g *caster sugar (135g plus 100g)*
2–3 *tablespoons warmed Apricot Glaze (page 147)*

A *few sugared almond slices*

**Apricots**
350g *no-need-to-soak dried apricots*
About 300ml *orange juice (to cover)*
1 *vanilla pod*
1 *cinnamon stick*
4 *cardamom pods*

First make the pastry. Sift the flour and icing sugar into a large bowl, mix in 25g of ground almonds then gradually work in 125g of the softened butter and 1 beaten egg to a smooth dough. Wrap in Clingfilm and chill for about 2 hours.

For the frangipane, simply cream together the 135g caster sugar, 135g butter, 135g almonds and 2 remaining eggs.

For the apricots, make a syrup with the 100g of caster sugar, the orange juice plus 100ml water. Bring to the boil with the spices. Add the apricots, return to a simmer and cook for about 10 minutes until softened. Cool in the syrup then drain. (The syrup can be used again).

Reserve 225g of the best fruits and purée the remainder in a blender or food processor.

Heat the oven to 160°C, Gas 3. Allow the pastry to return to room temperature then roll out to the thickness of a £1 coin (3mm). Cut out 8 rounds large enough to fill baby tartlet tins about 10cm in diameter. Leave to rest for 15 minutes then trim the tops.

Spread half the apricot purée on the base and place the whole apricots on top. Spoon over the frangipane, levelling the top. Place on a metal baking tray and bake for about 25 minutes until risen and golden brown. Remove from the oven and brush with apricot glaze. Cool then demould. Serve freshly baked with sugared almonds and scoops of Mascarpone on top and drizzle around the remaining purée.

## Alternative

Instead of tartlets, use the same ingredients and make a larger 30cm tart – wonderful for parties.

## Amaretto Mascarpone

*400ml Mascarpone*                    *50g icing sugar, sifted*
*5 tbsps Amaretto liqueur*

Whip together the Mascarpone, Amaretto and icing sugar. Chill until required and shape into quenelles using two dessert spoons. Place on top of each tart.

## Sugared Almonds

*100g caster sugar*                    *100g almond flakes*

Make a heavy sugar syrup by boiling together the sugar and 100ml water for 1–2 mins. Then drop in the almonds. Drain off the syrup and spread the coated nuts on a baking tray lined with a non stick silicone mat.

Heat the oven to 150°C, Gas 2 and bake for 8–10 mins until golden brown. Remove and cool. Store in an airtight tin until required.

# Lemon Tart with Almond Pastry

*Tangy yet creamy this is a classic French lemon tart perfect to end all dinners. Serve with a trickle of pouring cream or try our refreshing Lemon Sorbet (page 181) and top with a slice of Lemon Confit (page 26).*

Serves 8

| | |
|---|---|
| *180g plain flour* | **Filling** |
| *60g icing sugar plus 10g extra to caramelise* | *4 free range eggs* |
| *175g caster sugar* | |
| *1 small lemon, grated zest and half the juice* | *2 lemons, grated zest and juice* |
| *40g ground almonds* | *125ml double cream* |
| *85g butter, at room temperature* | *1 egg yolk, beaten with 1 teaspoon water* |
| *1 free range egg, beaten* | |

First, make the pastry. Sift the flour and 60g icing sugar together into a large bowl and mix in the lemon zest and ground almonds. Gradually work in the softened butter and the 1 beaten egg to a soft smooth dough. Wrap in Clingfilm and chill for about 2 hours.

For the filling, beat together the remaining 4 eggs and caster sugar until pale and creamy then mix in the remaining zest, lemon juice and cream.

Roll out the pastry to a round approximately 25cm and the thickness of a £1 coin (3mm). Lift on the rolling pin into a 20cm diameter loose bottomed flan tin, about 2cm deep. Press well into the sides and allow extra dough to overhang.

Leave to rest for about 15 minutes whilst you heat the oven to 180°C, Gas 4. Stand the pastry case on a baking tray, cover with foil and baking beans and bake blind for about 12 minutes. Remove the foil and beans, brush the base with egg yolk glaze and return to the oven for another 5 minutes. Then trim the overhanging pastry with a sharp knife to neaten. Cool.

Lower the oven to 140°C, Gas 1. Pour the lemon filling into the case and return to the oven for about 30 minutes until it is still slightly runny. Remove from the oven and set aside. The filling will set as it cools to room temperature.

To serve, cut the tart into 8 and dust each wedge thickly and evenly with 10g icing sugar. Light a cook's blow torch and caramelise the sugar. Serve at room temperature accompanied by scoops of Lemon Sorbet and Lemon Confit slices.

# Caramel Parfait Mille Feuille with Roasted Banana

*This looks like a super sophisticated ice cream wafer – slivers of caramel ice cream sandwiched between crisp brown sugar pastry layers topped with hot caramelised banana. You could make a simpler version though with just the parfait and hot bananas.*

Serves 6

*Caramel Sauce (page 147)*
*5 egg yolks*
*75g caster sugar*
*125ml double cream*
*About 200g Puff Pastry (page 144)*
*1 whole egg, beaten*
*Some caster sugar, to sprinkle plus*
  *30g for the bananas*

*20g butter*
*6 just ripe bananas, peeled*

**To serve**
*A few broken walnuts*
*6 dried banana slices (page 146),*
  *optional*

First make the Caramel Sauce. Set aside.

Then make the parfait. Place the yolks into an electric mixer set on a slow speed. Dissolve the sugar in about 3 tablespoons of boiling water. When dissolved, bring to the boil then cook to the soft ball stage (117°C on a cook's thermometer) – this takes about 5 minutes.

Remove and with the beaters whirling, pour the syrup onto the yolks and increase the speed to maximum. Beat until thick and pale golden then fold in half the Caramel Sauce along with the 125ml cream. Spoon into a shallow rectangular Swiss roll tin so the mixture is about 1cm thick. Freeze until solid.

Make the pastry wafers. Roll out the pastry as thin as possible. Using the rolling pin, lift onto a baking tray lined with non-stick baking parchment. Brush evenly with the beaten egg and sprinkle over an even layer of the sugar. Place another sheet of non-stick baking parchment and another baking tray on top. Leave to rest whilst you heat the oven to 180°C, Gas 4.

Bake for 10 minutes and uncover the top tray and sheet. Press the risen layers down to flatten and replace the paper and tray. Return to the oven for another 10 minutes until golden brown. Uncover and cool on a wire tray then using a very sharp knife cut out 12 wafers about 7 x 4 cm.

For the caramelised bananas, put the 30g of sugar into a hot pan with about 3 tablespoons of water. Dissolve over a low heat then raise the heat and cook to a light caramel colour. Remove from the heat and stir in the butter. Then return the pan to the heat and add the bananas, stirring well to coat in the sauce. Cook on a low heat, turning once or twice, carefully, until softened and golden. Keep warm.

To serve, lightly warm the remaining Caramel Sauce if necessary so it is runny. Spoon into a squeezy bottle and pipe zig zags on six dessert plates, or simply drizzle from a spoon.

Demould the parfait (the tin may have to be dipped for a few seconds into a bowl of hot water to loosen) and cut into six equal slices to fit the wafers. Sandwich together with the pastry wafers. Place these on top of the Caramel Sauce.

Cut each banana into 3 and place on top of the parfait sandwich slices. Scatter over the walnuts and, if liked, you could stick a roasted banana slice on top. Serve immediately.

# Passion Fruit Soufflés

*Add a touch of the exotic with these light tangy hot soufflés. The base can be made ahead and kept in the fridge. The secret of a successful sweet soufflé is to mix equal quantities of fruit base and meringue. They can be baked in ramekin dishes but we like to cook them in little soup or coffee cups. Perfect with scoops of homemade Coconut Ice Cream (page 181).*

Serves 8

*150ml passion fruit juice (from
  about 5–6 ripe wrinkled  fruits)
150ml fresh orange juice
3 large free range eggs, separated
240g (90g plus 150g) caster sugar*

*30g flour
A little melted butter
About 40g grated dark chocolate
A little icing sugar, sifted, to dust*

Boil together the passion fruit and orange juices for about 2 minutes. Meanwhile, beat together the egg yolks, 90g of the sugar and flour in a heatproof bowl. Pour on the hot juice and whisk together to blend then pour back into the saucepan and cook over a very low heart, stirring until it thickens. Cool, transfer to a bowl and chill until required.

Brush the insides of 8 large size ramekins or small bowls with melted butter then coat evenly in the chocolate and chill to set. (This helps the mixture rise up during baking). When ready to serve, heat the oven to 180°C, Gas 4.

Whisk the egg whites until forming soft peaks and then gradually whisk in the remaining 150g sugar. Transfer the chilled soufflé base to a large bowl and fold in the meringue. Divide between the ramekins and level the tops with the back of a knife.

Place the ramekins on a baking tray and bake for about 8 minutes until risen. Have a small sieve ready with the icing sugar and dust over the ramekins as they come out of the oven. Serve as quickly as you can before they start to sink gracefully. Serve with scoops of vanilla or Coconut Ice Cream on the side.

# Pistachio Crème Brûlées with Chocolate Sorbet

*I like to steep ground unsalted green pistachios in cream and milk for deliciously unusual crème brûlées. I like to serve them with scoops of Chocolate Sorbet (page 180) and Chocolate Sauce (page 146).*

### Serves 6

50g *unsalted, green pistachios,*
  *finely ground*
250ml *double cream*
250ml *milk*
5 *egg yolks*

65g *sugar*
*A little demerara sugar, for brûlée*
  *tops*
*Chocolate Sorbet, Chocolate Sauce*
  *and chocolate sticks, to serve*

Heat the ground nuts with the cream and milk until on the point of boiling. Cool and whiz in a liquidiser or food processor then strain the green milk through a sieve into a jug, pressing down on the nuts to extract the flavour and colour. Discard the nuts.

Beat the yolks and sugar in a heatproof bowl until thick and creamy. Reheat the green coloured milk to boiling and gradually pour onto the yolks beating to combine.

Heat the oven to 140°C, Gas 1. Place 6 medium ramekins in a roasting pan and pour in the custard. Pour boiling water around the dishes to make a bain-marie and bake for about 45 minutes until a skin forms and the mixture is still slightly runny. Remove and cool. The mixture will set as it cools.

Chill until required, then dredge the tops with demerara sugar and caramelise with a hot cook's blow torch. Serve with scoops of Chocolate Sorbet, Chocolate Sauce and chocolate sticks.

# Ice Cream Profiteroles

*There is a world of difference between shop profiteroles and home made. Ours are filled with small balls of homemade Luxury Vanilla Ice Cream (page 178) and coated with a hot Chocolate Sauce (page 146). They are so easy to make yourself, just prepare the choux buns, ice cream and sauce ahead of time and put together just before serving – heaven on a plate!*

Serves 8

| | |
|---|---|
| *150g plain flour* | *100g butter* |
| *¼ teaspoon sea salt* | *3 whole eggs* |
| *1 teaspoon caster sugar* | *Luxury Vanilla Ice Cream (page 178)* |
| *125ml milk* | *Chocolate Sauce (page 146)* |

Sift the flour, salt and sugar into a bowl. Put the milk, 125ml cold water and butter into a saucepan and bring to the boil. Tip in the flour in one go and stir vigorously with a wooden spoon until the mixture forms a soft dough that comes away from the pan sides.

Transfer the mixture to a bowl and cool for 5 minutes then gradually beat in 1 egg at a time until smooth. You may not need all the egg. Spoon into a piping bag fitted with a large plain nozzle.

Heat the oven to 190°C, Gas 5. Line a baking sheet with non-stick baking parchment or silicone sheet and pipe out 24 individual 3–4cm rounds. Bake for 10 minutes until risen and golden brown. For extra crisp buns, slit in half and pull out any soggy dough inside. Cool on a wire tray.

Make the Vanilla Ice Cream and Chocolate Sauce. Scoop the ice cream into small balls, the same number as the buns. These can be returned to the freezer until required laid out on a tray. Store in an airtight tin.

When ready to serve, place a scoop of ice cream into each choux bun. Allow 3 per serving, drizzle with the sauce and serve immediately.

# Earl Grey Prunes
# with Espresso Coffee Syrup

*Around Christmas time this becomes a popular menu choice at Simpsons. Spicy tea soaked prunes with a coffee syrup served with scoops of Armagnac Ice Cream, all of which can be made ahead. We like to use the plump French Agen prunes, even though they may need stoning after cooking. They have a far superior flavour and softer skins to others on the market.*

Serves 4

*250g Agen prunes, stoned*
*125g sugar*
*1 Earl Grey tea bag*
*$^1/_2$ cinnamon stick*
*1 vanilla pod*
*1 star anise*

*1 clove*
*Espresso Syrup (page 179)*
*Armagnac Ice Cream (page 182)*
*A few unsalted pistachios, chopped*
*    and some small mint sprigs*

Place all the ingredients from prunes to the clove in a large pan with 400ml water then bring slowly to the boil and simmer for 10 minutes. Tip into a bowl, cover and leave to infuse overnight.

Drain off the syrup, neatly reshape the prunes into neat ovals if necessary. Chill until required.

Make the coffee syrup and the ice cream. Serve all three together sprinkled with pistachios and mint sprigs.

# Rum Baba, Exotic Fruits and Crème Chantilly

*Rum babas are light sweet yeasty cakes soaked in rum syrup. We make ours in little deep moulds and serve them with fresh tropical fruits and more syrup. Serve with Crème Chantilly (see below).*

Serves 8

*15g fresh yeast (or 1 sachet fast action yeast)*
*100ml warm milk*
*230g plain flour*
*A good pinch sea salt*
*3 whole eggs, beaten*
*125g butter, softened to room temperature*
*Extra butter, melted for darioles*
*Some warmed Apricot Glaze (page 147)*

**Rum Syrup**
*140g caster sugar*
*1 strip lemon zest*
*1 strip orange zest*
*150ml dark rum*

**Exotic Fruits**
*100g caster sugar*
*1 cinnamon stick*
*1 vanilla pod*
*1 star anise*
*1 small pineapple*
*1 mango*
*1 papaya*
*2 kiwis*
*200g caster sugar*

If using fresh yeast, crumble it into the warm milk and stir until dissolved (do not do this with fast action yeast). Sift together the flour and salt into a deep bowl (stir in the fast action yeast at this point if using).

Mix in the warm milk and eggs to form a soft dough then gradually work in the softened butter. Cover with Clingfilm and leave in a warm spot in your kitchen (e.g. on top of your fridge or in an airing cupboard) until risen and doubled in volume. This can take up to 3 hours depending on the surrounding temperature.

Prepare the exotic fruits. Dissolve the 100g of sugar in 150ml of boiling water and add the whole spices. Infuse until cold, then remove the spices with a slotted spoon. Peel and stone the fruits as required and cut the pineapple, mango and kiwis into small neat 1cm dice. Slice the papaya into thin sticks. Reheat the syrup until almost boiling and pour over the fruits and leave until cold. Strain off the syrup.

Make the rum soaking syrup. Dissolve the 140g sugar in 200ml boiling water and simmer for 2 minutes. Add the zest strips, stir in the rum, remove from the heat and cool.

Brush 8 dariole moulds (100ml size) with melted butter to coat evenly. Knock back the risen dough and beat for a minute then spoon into a piping bag fitted with a large plain nozzle. Pipe into the prepared moulds about half full, place on a baking sheet and cover loosely with a sheet of Clingfilm lightly oiled. Allow to prove until risen just under the rim. Meanwhile, heat the oven to 200°C, Gas 6.

When the baba mixture is risen, remove the Clingfilm and bake on the tray for about 8 minutes until golden brown then remove and cool, then remove from the moulds, loosening with the tip of a knife. Put the babas in a deep sided dish and pour over the rum syrup. Leave to soak for about 10 minutes then strain off the syrup into a saucepan. This can be boiled down by half and served as a pouring sauce, if liked.

Brush the soaked babas with some warmed apricot glaze to make them shiny and serve with the fruits around and some Crème Chantilly alongside.

**Crème Chantilly**                    *1 vanilla pod*
*250ml double cream*                   *30g icing sugar*

Simply whip the cream with the vanilla seeds and sugar to soft peaks.

# White Chocolate Mousse with Raspberries and Coulis

*Perfect for summer, white chocolate mousse can accompany any of the summer berry fruits. To serve, I would suggest a simple coulis, and a light crisp tuile. We serve our mousses with a chocolate tuile but you could make a simpler Nut Tuile.*

Serves 4

*125g white chocolate*
*1 egg, separated*
*150ml double cream*
*300g fresh raspberries*

*1 teaspoon lemon juice*
*50g caster sugar*
*4 Nut Tuiles to serve (page 145)*

Break up the chocolate into a heatproof bowl and melt very gently either over a pan of barely simmering water or in the microwave on a low setting.

Beat the yolk with 2 teaspoons of water and mix with the melted chocolate then cool until tepid. Whilst the chocolate is cooling, whisk the egg white with a pinch of salt to soft peaks and set aside.

Whip the cream to soft peaks and fold in the whipped egg white then fold this mixture into the chocolate.

Spoon or pipe into ramekins or, for a more 'chefy' effect, set in a medium bowl and when firm, shape into quenelles using two dessertspoons to shape the mousse.

Make a coulis. Purée half the raspberries with the lemon and sugar and then rub through a sieve with the back of a ladle or wooden spoon.

To serve, mix half the coulis with the remaining raspberries. Serve the mousse with the raspberries and extra coulis drizzled around. Top each serving with a Nut Tuile.

# Ice Creams

Many of our ice creams are based on a classic crème anglaise custard – the method for which is similar throughout.
All ice creams make around 1 litre, enough for 6–8 servings.

## *Luxury Vanilla Ice Cream*

Makes just under 1 litre

*4 vanilla pods*          *6 egg yolks*
*450ml milk*              *120g sugar*
*150ml double cream*

Slit open the vanilla pods and scrape out the sticky seeds with the tip of a sharp knife. Put these into a saucepan with the milk, cream and the pods. Scald the milk and cream until on the point of boiling. Set aside and allow to cool a little, then remove the pods.

Beat the yolks and sugar together until thick, creamy and pale golden in a large heatproof bowl.

Reheat the vanilla milk and strain onto the beaten yolks. Whisk well then cool and chill.

Churn in an ice cream machine until firm, then scoop into a freezerproof container and freeze until required. Allow to thaw for 10 minutes before scooping.

# Tiramisu Ice Cream

325ml milk
175ml Amaretto liqueur
100ml espresso coffee or very strong
    hot coffee

6 egg yolks
100g caster sugar
A little Espresso Syrup (see below)

Boil the milk, Amaretto and 100ml of espresso coffee together and remove. Whisk together the yolks and sugar in a large heatproof bowl. Pour the hot milky coffee onto the sugar and yolks and whisk until thick.

Cool then churn in an ice cream machine until thick then scoop into a freezerproof container and freeze.

Allow the ice cream to thaw for about 10 minutes before serving. Serve with a little of the Espresso Syrup drizzled over the top.

## Espresso Syrup

200g caster sugar

100ml espresso coffee or very strong
    hot coffee

Dissolve the sugar with about 4 tablespoons of boiling water and boil to the soft ball stage, about 117°C. This takes about 10 minutes. Mix with the espresso coffee, cool and chill.

# Chocolate Ice Cream

200g dark chocolate, preferably
    60% cocoa solids
600ml milk

6 egg yolks
120g caster sugar

Break up the chocolate and place in a heatproof bowl. Boil the milk and pour over the chocolate, stirring until dissolved.

Beat together the yolks and sugar in a large heatproof bowl then gradually whisk in the hot chocolate milk. Strain back into the saucepan and stir over a very gentle heat until it starts to thicken.

Remove immediately from the heat and cool, then chill and finally churn in an ice cream machine. When thick, scoop into a freezerproof container and freeze until required. To serve, allow the ice cream to thaw for about 10 minutes then scoop to serve.

# Chocolate Sorbet

250ml milk
100g sugar
1/4 tsp sea salt

30g cocoa powder
200g Valrhona chocolate, (ideally
    Guanaja) broken in pieces

Heat together the milk, sugar, salt and cocoa powder with 250ml of water stirring until dissolved and on the point of boiling. Remove from the heat and add the chocolate, stirring until melted.

Cool to room temperature, stirring occasionally to stop a skin forming. Churn in an ice cream machine until thick then transfer to a freezerproof container and freeze. Thaw for 10 minutes before scooping into balls to serve.

# Sultana Ice Cream

150ml rum
150g sultanas
3 egg yolks

50g caster sugar
300ml milk

Boil the rum and pour over the sultanas then leave for two hours until they plump up.

Beat the yolks and sugar in a heatproof bowl until thick and creamy. Boil the milk and gradually pour onto the creamy yolks beating with a whisk, then return the mixture to the heat and cook over a very low heat stirring with a wooden spoon until the sauce thickens enough to coat the back of a spoon.

Remove, and stir in the soaked sultanas. Cool, then chill and churn in an ice cream machine until thick. Scoop into a freezerproof container and store until ready to serve. Thaw for about 10 minutes before scooping out to serve.

# Pain d'Epice Ice Cream

300ml milk
125g caster sugar

3 egg yolks
125g Pain d'Epice, diced (page 21)

Bring the milk just to the boil.

Whisk the sugar and egg yolks in a large heatproof bowl until thick and creamy. Pour the hot milk onto the egg yolks whisking continuously, then mix in the diced Pain d'Epice and stir until all ingredients are combined.

Cool, chill and churn in an ice cream machine until thick then transfer to a freezerproof container and freeze until required. Thaw for about 10 minutes before scooping to serve.

# Avocado Ice Cream

600ml milk
100g liquid glucose
6 egg yolks

200g sugar
2 ripe avocados
1 tablespoon fresh lemon juice

Heat the milk and glucose until dissolved and on the point of boiling. Remove from the heat.

Whisk the egg yolks and sugar in a large heatproof bowl until thick and creamy then gradually whisk in the hot sweet milk. Cool, chill then churn in an ice cream machine until thick.

Meanwhile, peel the avocados and mash or blitz with the lemon juice until creamy. When the ice cream is almost frozen, add the avocado purée and continue churning. Scoop into a freezer proof container and freeze until required. Thaw 10 minutes before scooping to serve.

# Lemon Sorbet

150g caster sugar
2 tbsp liquid glucose

Grated zest 1 lemon
150ml fresh lemon juice

Heat 125ml of water with the sugar and glucose until dissolved, then boil for 2 minutes

Remove from the heat and add the lemon zest and cool. When cool, stir in the juice, strain and churn in an ice cream machine until firm and slushy then transfer to a freezerproof container and freeze until required. Thaw 10 minutes or so before scooping.

# Coconut Ice Cream

6 egg yolks
175g sugar

1 x 400ml can coconut milk
200ml milk

Whisk the yolks and sugar in a large heat proof bowl until thick and creamy.

Bring the coconut milk and milk to boiling point then gradually pour onto the yolks, whisking as you pour. Return to the pan and on a very gentle heat stir with a wooden spoon until thickened enough to coat the back of a spoon.

Cool, stirring once or twice to stop a skin forming, then chill. Churn in an ice cream machine until thick then spoon into a freezerproof container and freeze. Thaw for about 10 minutes before scooping out.

# Armagnac Ice Cream

6 egg yolks                          250ml milk
175g sugar                           100ml Armagnac
250ml double cream

Beat the yolks and sugar together in a large heatproof bowl until thick and creamy.

Heat the cream and milk until on the point of boiling and gradually whisk into the yolk mixture.

Return the mixture to the saucepan and cook over a very gentle heat, stirring with a wooden spoon until it coats the back of the spoon. Remove, cool and chill then churn in an ice cream machine. As it begins to thicken add the Armagnac and continue churning.

Scrape into a freezerproof container and freeze until required. Allow to thaw 10 minutes before scooping.

# Acknowledgements

Whilst it's no easy task for a chef to do joined-up writing and write a book, I would like to say a special thank you to the following people who have supported and encouraged me through this endeavour.

Firstly, sincere thanks to Roz Denny for putting up with me and for her great skill and patience. Andrew Mobbs and his team for secretarial services. To Mark Law for food photography.

A chef is only as good as his brigade. I would like to give warm thanks to the guys that worked with me on this book – Luke Tipping, Adam Bennett, Ian Miller and Matt Cheal. I would also like to add a thank you to the suppliers for their support – Peter Allen of Aubrey Allen, Coventry; George Hicks from Birmingham veg market; and Channel Fisheries of Brixham.

And last of all, thanks to my dear wife Alison and to my children: Laura, Michael, Lisa and Sofia.